NOT SO FAR, FAR AWAY

Ancient Truths in a Modern Context

KEVIN MILLS
FOREWORD BY JEFF CRANSTON

Not So Far, Far Away
Ancient Truths in a Modern Context

© 2025 Kevin Mills
All rights reserved.

ISBN 979-8303618947

Milltown Press
Macon, Georgia

Printed in the United States of America

Scriptures taken from the Holy Bible, New International Version®, NIV®. Copyright © 1973, 1978, 1984, 2011 by Biblica, Inc.™ Used by permission of Zondervan. All rights reserved worldwide. www.zondervan.com The "NIV" and "New International Version" are trademarks registered in the United States Patent and Trademark Office by Biblica, Inc.™

*Dedicated to my parents, Bobby and Sue Mills,
who passed away in 2024 and 2022, respectively.
Thank you for everything.*

This is a work of fiction. Unless otherwise indicated, all the names, characters, businesses, places, events and incidents in this book are either the product of the author's imagination or used in a fictitious manner. Any resemblance to actual persons, living or dead, or actual events is purely coincidental.

CONTENTS

Foreword 7
Introduction
   Once upon a time, in a land far, far away..................... 9
Chapter 1: Barry's Billions
   The Parable of the Rich Fool 15
Chapter 2: Judah's Just Reward
   The Parable of the Unmerciful Servant........................ 37
Chapter 3: Sam's Two Sons
   The Parable of the Two Sons 65
Chapter 4: Penny's Pleas
   The Parable of the Persistent Widow 87
Chapter 5: Taylor's Treasure
   The Parable of the Hidden Treasure.......................... 111
Chapter 6: Steve's Scheme
   The Parable of the Shrewd Manager 139
Chapter 7: Caden's Curve
   The Parable of the Wise and Foolish Builders............. 159
Chapter 8: Mapleton's Murder
   The Parable of the Tenant Farmers........................... 185

FOREWORD

Is there any better way of teaching than storytelling? When terminology becomes technical and abstract, we easily tire. But a story! A picture painted with words has us leaning in, eagerly anticipating the next turn of events.

By way of the parables of Jesus, my fellow pastor Kevin Mills has graciously invited me to open the door to the "never-a-dull-moment" city of Mapleton. As a teacher, preacher, and author, he has already contributed outstanding efforts in all three categories, and once again, he gives literary expression to his thoughts. There is great wisdom in this. The printed page can be studied and considered far more than the spoken word can ever command.

Our author is a master storyteller, but this skill is more than a mere attention-getter. Like the parables of Jesus, the stories you are about to read are vessels for bringing the water of life to thirsty souls while at the same time, conveying the gospel truth.

"Every happening," writes Malcolm Muggeridge, "every happening, great and small, is a parable whereby God speaks to us." We can rejoice that Pastor Kevin has devoted his creative mind and solid exposition to expressing these noble stories of Jesus in a contemporary manner, introducing us to characters, some of whom we feel as if we have met somewhere before.

I believe you will not only enjoy but benefit, as I have, from his wonderfully imaginative narratives. You won't believe all that happens in Mapleton!

Jeff Cranston
Senior Pastor
LowCountry Community Church
Bluffton, South Carolina

INTRODUCTION

Once upon a time, in a land far, far away.

Many nights, on many occasions, I began the bedtime stories for my children with that phrase: *Once upon a time*. The sentences and paragraphs that followed contained harrowing tales of dragons, princes, and princesses. In these adventures, my children would ride into dangerous situations astride white stallions. They would battle evil dragons, wicked queens, villainous wizards, diabolic monsters, and even the occasional ornery opossum. All these mythical creatures would eventually be defeated and placed in the dungeon of the family castle. Then, everyone in the kingdom would celebrate with a pizza and ice cream party just before I uttered the closing words: *and they lived happily ever after*.

It's not just children who love a great story. There is something about a gripping narrative that captures our attention. We are drawn into the plot. We become advocates for the protagonist. We loathe the villain. We long for a happy ending. Or at least some measure of justice.

And, more notably, we *remember* the story. While a statement of fact may not stick to the roof of our brains for long, a good story is seared into our memories. We can recall, even years later, a well-crafted tale and the truths or morals contained within that narrative.

Which is why Jesus—the greatest teacher and preacher—was also the master storyteller. In fact, roughly one half to two-thirds of the teachings of Jesus were in the form of stories, or what are more commonly called *parables*. Contained within three of the four gospels (Matthew, Mark, and Luke) are between 35 and 65 unique parables. An exact number is difficult to determine. It depends upon how one classifies certain stories, and which ones are believed to be the same parable appearing multiple times in the gospels. However, it is estimated that we have about 40 parables of Jesus in the Bible. In his three years of teaching ministry on this earth I'm sure Jesus told many more, but these are the ones we have recorded.

Jesus not only captivated his audiences with these stories, but he also used the tales to convey profound truths. The moral lessons and guiding principles contained within these parables would stick with listeners for a long time. Instead of just offering a propositional truth or answering a question with a fact, law, or principle, Jesus would often tell a story.

When asked, "Who is my neighbor?" Jesus easily could have responded by saying, "Look around. People who are in need. Those are your neighbors."

Instead, Jesus told a powerful story about a Samaritan man coming to the aid of a wounded traveler. In that iconic tale, Jesus did more than just convey truth. He allowed his listeners to feel this reality in such a way that it would become lodged into their hearts. Never again did they have to ask themselves the question, "Who is my neighbor?" This story thrust the answer deep within their souls.

Many of these stories were so powerful, in fact, that they have become familiar references within popular culture. Even those who have never darkened the door of a church will refer to a helpful stranger as a *Good Samaritan*. A wayward child may very well receive the label, *Prodigal Son*, even from those who aren't very religious. The stories Jesus told and the truths they contain have lived on through history, becoming embedded within popular culture.

There are several reasons Jesus taught using parables. First, stories allow us to become emotionally invested in truth. If I tell you that you should help starving children around the world, you might respond, "I know. I should do something to help starving children."

But what if I tell you a story about an eight-year-old in Haiti named Josiah—a kid who loves soccer and has a million-dollar smile? Imagine me informing you that he is dying from malnutrition. I describe in detail his suffering, the limited resources available to his parents, and the fact that less than one American dollar per day would completely change his situation. You might have the same response as above; however, there is more conviction. The truth has moved from your head to your heart. You have become emotionally invested in living out what you intellectually know to be true.

Second, stories create an alternate universe with fictional characters and imaginative plots. They allow us to see what we already know to be true, but from a different angle and from the perspective of these make-believe characters. The story told by Nathan in 2 Samuel 12 allowed David to see his sin correctly. Previously, he'd been concerned only with his desires. The narrative provided a way for David to get outside of himself and see the truth of his sinful actions.

Third, stories can bring down our naturally defensive walls. Jesus used parables to call out individuals regarding their sin and hypocrisy. Tim Keller, in his book *The Prodigal God*, explains how a certain parable of Jesus angered the religious leaders listening to the story, yet they allowed him to condemn their actions in front of a crowd.[1] Had Jesus said to these men, "You have shown extreme disrespect for God through your elevation of the rules above people," they would have immediately closed their ears and walked away. Instead, they listened attentively as Jesus put their sin on full display.

Stories appeal to us. Everyone loves a well-spun yarn, a gripping narrative, and a tale as old as time. When terms, facts, and points have wearied us, a compelling illustration will breathe new life into our attention span.

Contained within these pages are eight familiar parables of Jesus, all modernized and set in the fictional town of Mapleton, located in the also fictional Grant County, Georgia.

---

[1] Timothy Keller, The Prodigal God: Recovering the Heart of the Christian Faith (New York: Dutton, 2008).

INTRODUCTION

In no way do I pretend to improve upon the parables of Jesus. They are *non-improvable*. However, sometimes the stories we read in the gospels seem too distant from our modern-day lives. There are sheep, shepherds, Samaritans, and scribes. The widows, bridegrooms, servants, and masters all "live in a land far, far away." The great chasm of centuries can make the settings feel ancient and unrelatable. With our modern ears, we sometimes miss the punchline of the story.

The following chapters are set in the present day. As you read these stories in a contemporary setting, perhaps you will see afresh the timeless truths Jesus conveyed.

Each story is coupled with a brief commentary on the parable as well as questions to aid in small group discussions. I pray we all learn a few things about ourselves as we dive into these tales from not so far, far away.

Kevin Mills
January 2025

CHAPTER 1

BARRY'S BILLIONS

The Parable of the Rich Fool

Someone in the crowd said to him, "Teacher, tell my brother to divide the inheritance with me."

Jesus replied, "Man, who appointed me a judge or an arbiter between you?" Then he said to them, "Watch out! Be on your guard against all kinds of greed; life does not consist in an abundance of possessions."

And he told them this parable: "The ground of a certain rich man yielded an abundant harvest. He thought to himself, 'What shall I do? I have no place to store my crops.'

"Then he said, 'This is what I'll do. I will tear down my barns and build bigger ones, and there I will store my surplus grain. And I'll say to myself, "You have plenty of grain laid up for many years. Take life easy; eat, drink and be merry."'

"But God said to him, 'You fool! This very night your life will be demanded from you. Then who will get what you have prepared for yourself?'

"This is how it will be with whoever stores up things for themselves but is not rich toward God."

Luke 12:13-21

A Few Comments...

Jesus told "The Parable of the Rich Fool" in response to a demand made upon him by someone in the crowd. Jesus was in the middle of a powerful sermon he delivered before an audience of thousands. In this message, Jesus focused on the goodness of God and God's intimate knowledge of our lives. "Therefore, do not worry or fear," Jesus said. "God's got you in the palm of his hand."

"Yeah, yeah!" someone in the crowd shouted. "All that's fine and nice, but I've got a much more important matter to discuss with you, Jesus! Tell my no good, rascally, cheating brother to share my part of the inheritance with me!"

Sigh. Evidently, not a single word of that sermon resonated with this man. Therefore, Jesus turned to his powerful, truth-communicating weapon: the parable. This story is of a wealthy man who suddenly becomes Uber-wealthy. His entire focus is on how much he has and how much more he can acquire. Yet, he passes away before he can enjoy this massive windfall. At the end of the parable and at the end of this man's life, the money meant nothing.

To drive the application point home, Jesus closed the parable with the following line: "So it will be for all who are focused on gaining money but aren't rich toward God." As he spoke these words, I imagine Jesus turned to the man who shouted the question, as if to say, "Maybe your brother owes you money, maybe he doesn't. However, you need to get your heart right before you pursue your claim on this inheritance."

There's not a lot of explanation needed for this parable. Jesus made his point abundantly clear. However, perhaps a modern-day story will shed a little more light on the truth Jesus communicated.

BARRY'S BILLIONS

In 2010, the U.S. Census Bureau determined that there were 28,652 souls residing in Grant County, Georgia, including 9,843 in Mapleton, the county seat and the largest of the three municipalities within the county. Located approximately sixty miles south- southwest of Atlanta and roughly forty miles from Columbus, Mapleton had three elementary schools, one middle school, and one high school. It was the kind of place where most everyone knew most everyone else and most everyone else's business. Secrets never remained secrets for long in Mapleton.

That same year, the estimated average annual household income of Grant County was just under $38,000. However, that statistic certainly didn't apply to Bartholomew Hawthorn Sanders, Jr., *a.k.a.*, Mr. Barry. He was, by millions of dollars, the wealthiest resident of Grant County. Although unprovable, most believed he was the richest man in all of Central and South Georgia. Sure, there were businessmen and pro athletes in the big city of Atlanta who had more money, but probably not in Columbus, Macon, Valdosta, or even Savannah. Well, maybe Savannah, but not those other cities.

You see, Mr. Barry wasn't just wealthy. He was superrich. He had his own plane he kept parked at a private airport near Columbus. Rumors swirled around town that he owned a yacht docked at an exclusive marina in Destin, Florida. However, Mr. Barry would never confirm nor deny this fact when asked. Truthfully, he spoke very little about his personal life. Mr. Barry was, as they say, "all business," and he was very good at what he did.

His particular area of expertise—and the source of his tremendous wealth—was plastic chairs. Chairs used in school cafeterias and auditoriums across the United States. His father, the first Bartholomew Sanders, established Sanders Seating in the early 1960s. After the birth of his firstborn, father and son became known as Big Barry and Little Barry, respectively. Barry Jr. always hated this designation and the feeling of living in his father's shadow. After graduating from the University of Georgia in 1992, Little Barry wanted to do anything other than work for his dad. However, the country was in the middle of an economic recession, and his options were few. He swore that he would stay for only a few years—until he could save enough money and move to some place where he was the only Bartholomew Sanders in town, and nobody called him "Little."

However, after just two years of employment at the factory, his plans unexpectedly changed. Big Barry, at only 51 years old, suffered a massive heart attack one Saturday morning while playing golf at the local country club. To this day, there is a wrought iron park bench next to the sixteenth green, the place where Big Barry collapsed after sinking a ten-foot putt for birdie. The commemorative plaque on the bench is dedicated to Bartholomew "Big Barry" Sanders.

Suddenly, 25-year-old Little Barry became the CEO of Sanders Seating. Irene Sanders, the widow and mother of Little Barry, was technically the owner. However, she had zero interest in running the business. As long as she received a monthly check with enough funds to keep her in the lifestyle to which she had become accustomed, she was happy to let her son run the operation.

Turns out that Little Barry (who now insisted his employees call him Mr. Barry) had a real knack for business. Since he was unmarried and had zero hobbies, he was able to put in 12 to 15 hours a day at the company. While his father had been content to do things as they had always been done, Barry introduced new and improved machinery, processes, and marketing ideas. He purchased badly needed, modernized equipment. He developed methods to enhance production, and nearly doubled the number of chairs manufactured in a week without adding one employee to the payroll.

More importantly, he spent hours on the phone, calling nearly every school district's central office from Virginia to Louisiana. Although Barry was short, overweight, and prematurely bald, he had a magnificent voice. His accent was southern, but not country. On the phone, he sounded almost aristocratic. *Distinguished* was a word often used by those who spoke with Barry on the phone, but not so much by those who talked with him face-to-face.

But his voice did the trick. Plus, his new production methods allowed him to undercut prices of the competition. Within a couple of years after his father's death,

Barry was sending trucks from Grant County, Georgia, all across the southeast. Plastic chairs with small, raised letters spelling out *Sanders Seating* sat in thousands of school lunchrooms, auditoriums, libraries, and gymnasiums. Barry chuckled to himself as he thought about how much bigger Sanders Seating was now that "Little Barry," not "Big Barry," ran the company. "This'll show them," he thought, "who the big guy really is."

As his company grew, so did his fortunes. Three weeks after Barry's 32nd birthday, his mother died, and not only did he inherit her fortune, but he also no longer had to send her a portion of the company's monthly profit. When he turned 35, his net worth exceeded $100 million. Barry and his accountant were the only two individuals who knew this information.

That same year, Barry placed an ad online for a marketing assistant. Ashley Barrows, a recent graduate of the University of Georgia, mailed her resume to Mr. Barry Sanders' attention at the company and—after a month with no reply—made the hour's drive from her parents' house in Marietta to Mapleton. She walked into the office doors just as Barry was headed out to lunch. Although it was often said that the only thing Barry thought attractive was a stack of Benjamins, he was immediately mesmerized by Ashley Barrows. She smiled at him with her gleaming white, perfect teeth, then flung her radiant blonde hair to one shoulder. Ashley introduced herself and said that she was inquiring about the status of the marketing position. Barry invited her into his office, quickly found her resume in a scattered stack of papers, asked her a few questions, and hired her on the spot. She told him that she would be able to start the next Monday and would commute from her parent's home in Atlanta until she could find an apartment in Mapleton. As she walked out of his office, Barry knew he was in trouble.

Exactly eight months later, Ashley quit her job to devote her full-time attention to the upcoming wedding. Six months after that, she and Barry Sanders were married on a farm just outside of Marietta. Although not all were invited, hundreds of Mapleton's citizens showed up to witness their town's most eligible bachelor tying the knot.

Ten years and two children later, Barry Sanders found himself working just as hard and making more money than even he had imagined possible. He rarely saw Ashley and the kids. None seemed to mind all that much. They had a full-time nanny and a part-time cook. Ashley spent most of her days playing tennis, going to lunches with friends, and attending meetings of various clubs. She had no clue how much money she and Barry had in the bank; all that mattered was that she wanted for nothing.

According to the ever-running, rarely reliable Mapleton rumor mill, it was a group of teenage hoodlums who started the fire. However, when the police asked the residents of the homes located within eyesight of First

Baptist, no two stories matched. Mrs. Johnson claimed that she thought she saw two "suspicious-looking boys" running through the Hillbrook's front yard, sprinting away from the church and down the street toward the old mill village. However, Mr. Hillbrook told the police officer that he and Sammy Underwood were training for a 10K, and that they had just completed a five-mile run around dusk. "And, no, we didn't see any suspicious boys. And, by the way, Mrs. Johnson can't see much past the end of her nose. I'm pretty sure it was me and Sammy she saw."

A few other accounts given by neighbors raised suspicions of arson. But, a few days later, the fire inspector put all those rumors to bed when he determined the actual cause of the fire—a faulty electrical panel. The severely outdated wiring at First Baptist had been, for years, a neglected maintenance item. The cost to rewire the old building was way too steep, and, as had been mentioned in more than one business meeting, everything was working just fine. "If it ain't broke, don't fix it" was the opinion of the majority.

Except, the outdated electrical system had caught the attention of the insurance representative some years earlier, leading to a specific exclusion in the church's property insurance policy.

The massive, four-alarm fire completely destroyed the educational building. Fortunately, a covered walkway connected that building to the sanctuary, keeping the fire from causing any further damage. Three weeks later, a general contractor—who also happened to be a member of First Baptist—delivered the bad news to Pastor Henry Miller. "Even if I cut the percentage of what I take to the bone, a new education building will cost at least $3 million. More if the church wants high-end finishes."

Pastor Miller took this information to the board of deacons. First Baptist was, and had been for decades, a debt-free church. He knew these men would have little interest in borrowing money for the project. As he suspected, they voted to raise the money and, once the cash was in hand, they would rebuild the educational building.

The first Sunday in October was designated as, "First Fruits Sunday." Members had already made pledges toward the project totaling just over $2.5 million. The deacons had reluctantly agreed to secure a short-term loan and to start on the project if the church could have a million dollars in the bank. They would borrow the remaining amount needed to finish the project with the hopes of quickly paying off the debt.

This decision by the deacons meant that "First Fruits Sunday" would determine whether the contractor would begin immediately rebuilding the educational space or if there would be a delay. Pastor Henry Miller used every tool at his disposal to encourage the members to give "substantially and sacrificially" toward this project.

One significant step had been to contact Mr. Barry and request a meeting. Although Barry Sanders hadn't attended First Baptist Church since his mother's funeral, his name was on the membership roll. He and some friends came to the church's annual Vacation Bible School the summer after Barry's fourth grade year. Three of his classmates and "Little Barry" all professed to become Christians on the last day and were baptized that following Sunday. Barry's family attended only sporadically for the next few months, and then rarely in the years that followed that experience. Barry felt like going to church was a waste of his time, especially with the ever-present demands of his company.

However, he was technically a member of the church. More significantly, Barry Sanders was, by miles, the wealthiest member of the community. Pastor Miller managed to secure a meeting with Barry at his office on the Tuesday before "First Fruits Sunday." The pastor explained the details of the project and just how difficult it would be to continue ministering to families without the educational space. They needed the construction to begin ASAP and that would require the church to have $1,000,000 in hand. Would he prayerfully consider coming to church on that Sunday and making a financial gift?

Barry agreed, partially just to end the meeting so he could get back to work. As well, he knew that he actually would consider giving toward the rebuilding of the educational space. It was in that old, now burned-and-collapsed building where he made the decision to become a Christian. Although it wasn't currently an important factor in his life, Barry had a sense of nostalgia when it came to the church in general and the educational space in particular. He would think about it and come up with a number.

That following Sunday afternoon, Henry Miller contacted Charlie Thompson, the chairman of the deacons, to share with him the great news. "Charlie, you won't believe it, but the total is just over $1.3 million. It's the largest single-Sunday offering in the history of First Baptist Church. I'm calling the contractor tomorrow. I'm hoping he can get started this week."

"Pastor, that is amazing. No one thought we would collect that much. If you don't mind, can I ask you if there were any extraordinarily large gifts?"

"Yes, there was one. Of course, I don't know the amounts anyone gave. Norma never shares that information. She did say that one check was for a million dollars. And Charlie, between me and you, I went to visit with Barry Sanders last week and asked him to consider donating toward this project. And I'm glad I did. I saw him Sunday at church. And when I asked people to bring the envelopes with their offering to the altar and place them in the basket, Barry walked down and dropped his in. If I were a betting man, I would guess that was the source of the million-dollar check. I think that meeting with him was certainly worth my time."

Norma Smith was the financial secretary at First Baptist Church, a position she'd held for over thirty years. And Norma was a vault when it came to revealing any names connected to giving. If a member made a statement of fact about another member's financial contribution, Norma would neither confirm nor deny the truthfulness of the claim. She had learned to master the art of the poker face and kept in complete confidence any and all information regarding tithes and offerings given to First Baptist Church.

Norma was the only person, other than Barry, who knew the actual amount of his gift on "First Fruits Sunday." After Pastor Miller left his office, Barry looked over his financial statements. His estimated worth was just under $800 million. His unstated yet firm goal was to become a billionaire before he turned 50. When his mother passed away thirteen years earlier, the thought of reaching that elite status entered his mind and stuck with him. Every day he mentally calculated how much more he needed to cross the finish line. While his wife's spending did slow his progress, he had managed to continue adding to his net worth every year. So that now, at 45 years old, he was only $200 million away from reaching his goal.

Barry thought about Henry's words regarding the building project and the hope of having enough money to begin construction immediately. During their conversation, Barry asked the pastor about the number of members at First Baptist. "Just over a thousand," he said. "Although, you know, the FBI and Post Office combined would have trouble finding some of them." Henry winced as he thought about the fact that Barry was one of those perpetually absent names on the membership roll.

Barry did some quick calculations. One thousand members. If every member would give a certain amount, then the goal could be realized.

That is how Barry determined to write a $1000 check to First Baptist Church.

As well, Norma was the only person, other than Mrs. Johnson, who knew the source of the $1 million check. When her husband died fifteen years earlier, Mrs. Johnson received a sizable life-insurance payment. She and her husband were always comfortable, but never wealthy. Mr. Johnson spent most of his career working as a shop teacher at the local high school. They lived in a modest home just across the street from First Baptist Church. Her two children were grown, married, had children of their own, and both lived in Atlanta.

Until she opened the envelope labeled, "Only Open If I'm Dead," she had no idea of the existence of this policy and the $1.5 million check she would receive from the American Mutual Life Insurance Company. She immediately invested the money, spent very little, and now, at 85 years old, was worth nearly $4 million. She had more than enough for her needs and plenty to leave her children and grandchildren. Plus, she dearly loved both her Lord and the church where she went to worship. Mrs. Johnson pledged $2 million to the campaign and gave a $1 million check on the "First Fruits Sunday."

NOT SO FAR, FAR AWAY

On the morning of his 46th birthday, Barry didn't feel much like celebrating. He woke up thinking about his life, his company, and his assets. He felt as if he'd hit a financial ceiling. Although he had made a lot of progress over the years, he had struggled recently to reach his goal of becoming a billionaire. His net worth was increasing, but at a slower pace. Anxiety filled his heart and mind about the possibility of waking up in 4 years, on his 50th birthday, and being incredibly disappointed.

However, it wasn't in his nature to sit around and sulk. Barry's mantra in life had always been to grab the bull by the horns, lift yourself up by your own bootstraps, make your own way, or whatever other platitude one uses to indicate hard work and success.

And the more he thought about it, the more he realized what he had to do. To have the kind of financial prosperity he desired, he needed to get out of Mapleton and Grant County. He had to move to a place where he could build a larger manufacturing plant and have access to a more substantial labor force. All the big, successful companies were based in major metropolitan areas, not little towns like Mapleton. Becoming a billionaire would require him to move his operations to Atlanta.

Barry was exhausted, but it was a good kind of tired. He'd spent all day at the architect's office in Atlanta. After countless hours of discussion and reviewing numerous concepts, this architect finally understood Barry's vision. The design documents were complete. Assuming there were no hiccups with planning and zoning, they would begin construction within the month on his new manufacturing complex. He planned to break the news to Ashley the next morning. They would be moving to Atlanta soon. He would have to be clear, as well, that she absolutely could not tell a soul. If word leaked out that he was moving Mapleton's second-largest employer (the public school system being the biggest) to Atlanta, his name would be mud. More importantly, he might lose employees and, thus, production time. It was critical that this move remained secret. That is, until the new plant was up-and-running.

But that conversation was for tomorrow. Tonight, he would allow himself a stiff drink as he pored over the blueprints. As he turned each page, he became more and more excited about this new, larger, and more efficient manufacturing plant. He knew—*he just knew*—that this was the right move. This new chapter in the history of Sanders Seating would propel him to the next level of wealth and status in this world.

In fact, as he continued to dream, a fresh thought entered his mind. Sure, reaching billionaire status would be a slam-dunk in this new facility. But why stop there? Could he make another billion before turning 55? Probably, if he worked hard and with just a little luck. That was his new goal: a net worth of $2 billion by 55.

Barry's *billions*. With an *s*. Yeah, he liked the sound of that.

It was around 7:00 a.m. when Ashley emerged from her bedroom and walked downstairs, wondering why her husband had not come to bed the night before. He'd arrived home late from some out-of-town meeting, excited but with zero interest in talking. The family ate dinner without him. She offered some leftovers. Their cook, Rosie, had prepared beef bourguignon for her and Barry and, as usual, spaghetti for the kids. He politely, but quickly, declined. She could tell he was anxious to get to his home office and work. This was not unusual; however, tonight he was especially intent on wrapping up their conversation so he could focus on work matters.

Ashley peeked her head into his office. The morning sun wiggled its way through the blinds, casting enough light into the room for Ashley to see her husband seated in his chair. There he was, at his desk, slumped over and resting his head on a mound of scattered papers.

She walked over and gently placed her hand on his back. "Wake up," she whispered. "Go up to bed and get a couple hours of sleep. It's Saturday. Maybe you could spend it with me and the kids?" She knew it was a foolish question. He would quickly eat breakfast and offer some reason why his presence was demanded at the plant.

But just maybe, she thought, since he'd spent the night working, he might find a little time for the family today.

"Barry, what do you think?" she asked. No response. Barry didn't budge. "Honey, you fell asleep at your desk. Go get in the bed." Still, nothing. Ashley again placed her hand on his back and lightly shook him. "Barry?" she said with a little more volume and force. When he still did not respond, she shook him again, this time with substantial effort. His head and shoulders slid across the desk, and his body followed, out of the chair and onto the floor. Ashley stood over him and suddenly understood the reality of the situation.

Mr. Barry Sanders was dead.

First Baptist Church of Mapleton was completely packed on that Wednesday afternoon. Although the pews comfortably held 600 individuals, over 900 managed to squeeze themselves in for this occasion. Men stood, lining the walls in the back of the room, the sides, and in the balcony. Individuals filled every seat in the choir loft. A few chairs were placed in the foyer and, with the doors open, those seated could mostly hear and somewhat see the various elements of the service.

Pastor Miller, it was later stated, delivered the best funeral message of his life. He used the parable of the talents and tied it directly to the life of Mr. Barry Sanders.

He spoke eloquently about Barry's contributions to the community and how his company had brought economic blessings to Mapleton. Pastor Miller also mentioned his recent meeting with Barry and alluded to Barry's generosity toward the church. Most members of the church knew there had been a significant contributor to the recent fundraising campaign, and assumed it was Barry Sanders. They nodded their heads in agreement with the pastor's comments.

The funeral service ended, and the pallbearers carried the casket out of the sanctuary and loaded it into the back of the hearse. The vehicle procession was like none the town had ever seen. The hearse and limousines were escorted by four state patrol cars to the cemetery. Almost all who attended the church came to the graveside service. Pastor Miller spoke again, although his remarks were brief. He closed by reading Psalm 23.

The crowd milled around for a while, offered their condolences to Ashley and the kids, made comments about the wonderful tribute to Barry, wondered aloud about the future of Sanders Seating, and eventually began to disperse.

After everyone left, three men lowered the coffin into a cement vault, sealed it, and used their shovels to fill the hole with dirt. Once finished, they placed a large marker in the ground. Engraved on the tombstone were the following words:

Bartholomew Hawthorn Sanders
October 5, 1970—July 29, 2017
Loving Husband and Father
"Well done, thy good and faithful servant."

The men loaded the funeral tent and chairs into the back of a large truck and exited through the gates of the Memorial Gardens Cemetery. A few hours later, the sun finished its daily descent, and darkness covered Mapleton.

Just after midnight, an angel of the Lord entered through the cemetery gates and quietly weaved his way through the collection of grave markers. Eventually, he found the gravesite of Mr. Barry Sanders. For several minutes, he stood and studied the words written on the tombstone.

Then, over the engraving, the angel took his heavenly finger and inscribed one word:

FOOL

QUESTIONS FOR DISCUSSION:

Ice-Breaker: If you won a $100 million in the lottery, how would you spend the money?

1. What are some similarities between this story and the parable of Jesus? Differences?
2. Do you believe Barry was a Christian? Why or why not?
3. Why did the angel write "fool" over Barry's tombstone? Similarly, why did God call the man a fool in the parable?
4. Was it wrong for Barry to be wealthy? Why or why not?
5. Look back at verse 21 in the parable? What is the warning in this verse? How did Barry (and the rich fool) not heed this warning?
6. Read I Timothy 6:7. What does this verse say is a danger of wealth? Why is it such a temptation to put hope in wealth?
7. Read Matthew 6:19-21. What do these verses say about our hearts and money? How can we keep ourselves from becoming too attached to our money?
8. Read 2 Corinthians 9:6-8. What do these verses say about generosity?
9. Read Malachi 3:8-12. What do these verses say about tithing? What is tithing? Is this something you practice? Why or why not?

CHAPTER 2
JUDAH'S JUST REWARD
The Parable of the Unmerciful Servant

Then Peter came to Jesus and asked, "Lord, how many times shall I forgive my brother or sister who sins against me? Up to seven times?"

Jesus answered, "I tell you, not seven times, but seventy-seven times.

"Therefore, the kingdom of heaven is like a king who wanted to settle accounts with his servants. As he began the settlement, a man who owed him ten thousand bags of gold was brought to him. Since he was not able to pay, the master ordered that he and his wife and his children and all that he had be sold to repay the debt.

"At this the servant fell on his knees before him. 'Be patient with me,' he begged, 'and I will pay back everything.' The servant's master took pity on him, canceled the debt and let him go.

"But when that servant went out, he found one of his fellow servants who owed him a hundred silver coins. He grabbed him and began to choke him. 'Pay back what you owe me!' he demanded.

"His fellow servant fell to his knees and begged him, 'Be patient with me, and I will pay it back.'

"But he refused. Instead, he went off and had the man thrown into prison until he could pay the debt. When the other

servants saw what had happened, they were outraged and went and told their master everything that had happened.

"Then the master called the servant in. 'You wicked servant,' he said, 'I canceled all that debt of yours because you begged me to. Shouldn't you have had mercy on your fellow servant just as I had on you?' In anger his master handed him over to the jailers to be tortured, until he should pay back all he owed.

"This is how my heavenly Father will treat each of you unless you forgive your brother or sister from your heart."

Matthew 18:21-35

A Few Comments...

Following a discussion on how to handle sin within the church, Peter asked Jesus a pointed question: "How many times do I have to forgive someone who has sinned against me?" In other words, is there a limit to the mercy I am required to show toward the person who has wronged me?

Peter followed up his question with a suggested number: "Up to seven times?" Peter was likely looking for an *attaboy* from Jesus. "Wow, that's quite noble of you. Forgiving someone who has hurt you that many times puts you in a religiously elite category. Way to go, Peter."

Instead, Jesus responded with a shocking statement. "Not seven, but seventy-seven times." Some translations read, "Seventy times seven," or 490 times forgiving the person who hurt you. In other words, forgiveness should be a deep well that never runs dry.

On the heels of this statement, Jesus told the above parable, a gripping story of a servant who owes a king more money than he could earn in a thousand lifetimes. The king orders this man to be tossed into prison and his wife and children sold into slavery to pay back a portion of the debt. The man pleads for mercy, insisting that he will pay the debt if he has just a little more time. Of course, this was impossible. The man could never pay what he owed to the king. Yet, this king shows incredible mercy. Instead of tossing this man in prison, he completely cancels the debt owed. Imagine the feeling of freedom one would experience after having several million dollars fully forgiven.

Except, this man apparently had a bad case of short-term memory loss. He leaves the king's presence, only to see a man who owes him a hundred bucks, or roughly a day's wages. This servant demands immediate payment. When the man is unable to do so, the servant has him thrown into prison. Word gets back to the king about what has happened, and this king is furious. He showed incredible mercy to the servant, but this same servant could not show just a little mercy to his neighbor. The king then has the man tortured and thrown into prison.

Just in case his listeners didn't understand the point, Jesus made the application crystal clear: "This is how my heavenly Father will treat each of you unless you forgive your brother or sister from your heart" (Matthew 18:35).

Wow. That statement should scare us. It's quite sobering. If we don't forgive, then we will be tortured and thrown into prison?

Don't let this parable lead you into legalism. The point of Jesus wasn't that a person who fails to forgive one time will be cast into hell. Do not become overwhelmed with thinking that you must fully forgive every person who has ever hurt you, and if you fall short you will not receive forgiveness from your Heavenly Father. That would be a works-based salvation and run right against the grain of the gospel.

The main point of Jesus in this parable is that Christians should be bent toward forgiveness. When you read the story, it seems foolish that this servant would demand the $100 payment from his neighbor. It's hard to imagine anyone having millions of dollars forgiven and immediately becoming enraged over someone not paying them the few dollars they were owed.

This is the theme of the story. Christian, you have been forgiven an enormous debt, one you could never, ever repay. How, then, can you not forgive others? The person who isn't willing to forgive most likely has never truly experienced the forgiveness of Jesus.

Perhaps a story about Judah Stephens will shed a little more light on this truth.

JUDAH'S JUST REWARD

Mapleton's proudest moments as a community came in two forms. One was any year in which the Mapleton High School football team advanced to the state playoffs. When this occurred, conversations in restaurants, homes, workplaces, churches, and especially at the high school, would revolve around the details of the upcoming matchup between Mapleton and whoever stood in the way of their title. The 1996 team made it to the championship game but suffered a heartbreaking loss. The 1979 and 2001 squads played in and won the state championship. Those teams and their seasons offered spectacularly proud moments for Mapleton and left indelible memories in the minds of her citizens.

The second point of pride was the annual Maple Festival, which happened in October every year. Mapleton derived her name from the Japanese maple tree. Thousands of these trees dotted the community and, more notably, symmetrically lined a two-mile stretch of Main Street. From the business district, past several churches, and down through a residential area, these trees sat just to the right of the sidewalk, spaced exactly fifteen feet apart. Every fall, the leaves of these trees turned a stunningly bright red. The week-long festival celebrating this natural transformation included a parade, an arts-and-crafts fair, a crowning of the maple tree queen, and a festival-ending band party at the community park located on Main Street. Visitors traveled from Atlanta, Columbus, and Macon to attend these events and walk or drive the two-mile stretch of Main Street, admiring the two impressive red columns created by the maple leaves.

Unless the football team made the state playoffs, this was the annual highlight for the community.

Judah Stephens lived on Main Street in a three-bedroom, two-bath bungalow constructed in 1921. He and his wife purchased the home in 1986 for $42,000. Thirty years later, the house was estimated to be worth five times what they'd paid; however, Judah had no interest in selling. At 60, he was only a few years away from retirement, and he planned to leave his home only if it was feet first, on a gurney, carried out by two employees of the local funeral home.

Judah worked as the controller for Grant County, a position he'd held since moving to Mapleton thirty years prior. As controller, he was responsible for overseeing the income and expenditures for the county, as well as insuring that this data was properly recorded in accordance with *Generally Accepted Accounting Principles*, then presented to county officials in a timely manner. His work was detailed and considered by others to be tedious and boring.

But not to Judah. He loved numbers. Unlike people, they never disappointed him. They didn't have feelings or bad days. They didn't create office drama. Invoices never called in sick. A balance sheet wouldn't not do its job because of a morning fight with its spouse. A budget document never claimed it was late because of traffic. As long as he did his job correctly, a P&L would as well.

As much as he loved his job, he faithfully left the office every afternoon at precisely 4:00 p.m. He made the five-minute drive to his home and parked in his perfectly organized, detached, two-car garage. Judah then changed out of his business attire and into his gardening clothes. He would make his way to the outdoor shed on the back of his property to retrieve whatever tools he needed to tackle his latest horticultural endeavor. Unless prohibited by weather or the wintertime absence of daylight, Judah spent 1-2 hours every afternoon caring for his lawn, shrubs, and flowers. He then showered, changed, and by 7:00 p.m. was seated next to his wife on the couch in their den. Their respective dinners sat on television trays as they watched *Wheel of Fortune* and *Jeopardy!* Most nights, Judah went to bed early so he could be seated at his office desk by 7:00 a.m. the next morning.

His daily gardening routine wasn't without effect. The Stephens had, unquestionably, the most beautiful yard on Main Street. Not one weed could be spotted in his Zoysia grass cut to exactly two and a half inches high. His nearly one hundred running feet of road frontage gave him six Maple trees, all with perfectly manicured beds surrounding each base. Encore azaleas encircled his home. A raised bed along his driveway boasted colorful annuals throughout the year—pansies in the winter and a combination of vincas and begonias during the spring and summer. Judah typically planted yellow and orange marigolds in the fall.

However, the *pièce de résistance* of his yard was the cluster of hydrangea shrubs lining the fence between his property and Mrs. Johnson's. Every June, these plants would explode with bright blue blossoms. For a solid three months, anyone driving down Main Street and headed out of town would witness this blue and green masterpiece painted against a tall, wooden fence. Neighbors strolling down the sidewalk would often stop and gawk at the flowers, in perfect bloom, set against the healthy green leaves of thriving plants.

Judah was often asked for the secret to his care of these temperamental shrubs and, more often, how in the world he got the blooms to such a radiant color of blue? He would simply shrug his shoulders as he replied, "I'm not really sure. Just lucky, I guess."

But luck had nothing to do with it. Only he and Mrs. Stephens knew the magical key to his horticultural success: *coffee grounds.* Every morning, Judah's wife removed the used grounds from their coffee filter and emptied them into a container kept in their laundry room. Once every couple of weeks, Judah scattered the grounds around his thirty precious shrubs. Throughout the year, he carefully tended to these plants by adding soil, pulling out any pesky weeds, pruning, and spreading mulch to hold in the moisture. Then, each summer, his yard became the showpiece of Mapleton. Ironically, as much as Judah didn't care for people, he wanted them to be impressed with yard.

And they were.

Every spring, the Mapleton City Auditorium held a large gathering of teenagers who came from across the county. *Springfest* always featured the performance of a contemporary Christian musician punctuated by personal testimonies of a few brave high schoolers who were willing to stand before their peers and talk about their respective faith journeys. The pinnacle of the event was a sermon from a well-known Christian speaker. This evangelistic message called for unsaved students to make a decision for Christ, and every year, there were dozens—one year over a hundred—who professed Jesus as their personal Lord and Savior. Pastors and youth pastors spent weeks and months preparing for *Springfest*. For twenty years, their annual efforts were not in vain. Churches and youth groups saw great fruit resulting from this county-wide event.

The second largest incorporated municipality in Grant County, Rockdale, had traditionally been Mapleton's chief high school sports rival. Most gatherings of citizens from each town were filled with tension over the performances of their football, basketball, and baseball teams. However, at *Springfest*, foes became friends and one in Christ, praying together for the spiritual renewal of Grant County.

At *Springfest 2015*, an 11th grade student from Rockdale gave her testimony. Cassie Ford, the previous year, had suffered through the loss of her mom to cancer. The crowd of nearly 1,000 high school and middle school students listened intently as she talked about her family's tragic journey, the heartbreak of losing her mom and best friend, and the inexplicable peace she found through her faith in Christ. Besides Cassie's voice, the only other sound heard during her time on stage were the suppressed sniffles of both girls and guys.

While everyone listened to Cassie, Drew Cashwell, a junior at Mapleton High School, focused more steadfastly than the others. Eight years earlier, when Drew was in elementary school, he'd lost his father. Drew's dad, whom everyone called "Cash," worked the second shift at a tire factory located about thirty minutes north of Mapleton. Coming home from work late one night, Cash fell asleep at the wheel, ran off the road, and wrapped his car around a tree. He died instantly.

Not only was Drew drawn to Cassie because of their shared experiences, but he also thought she was the most beautiful girl he'd ever seen. As she spoke, he honestly believed she gleamed like an angel. Later, she would inform him that it was the theatrical stage lighting that gave him this impression; however, it didn't matter. Before she ended her remarks that evening, Drew was completely smitten.

At the conclusion of *Springfest*, Drew managed to worm his way through the mob of students to find Cassie. He nervously introduced himself, told her how much he enjoyed hearing her speak, and mentioned that he'd also lost a parent a few years earlier. Her friends told her it was time to leave, and so he quickly said, "And if you'd be interested, I'd love to get together sometime and talk more about what we've been through."

As friends pulled her away, Cassie smiled at Drew and said, "Message me."

That night, he did. And she responded. The conversation continued online until Drew asked for her phone number. Drew called Cassie on Sunday, and they talked for a couple hours. Before the conversation ended, he asked her for a date on Friday. She agreed. He drove to Rockdale in his mom's ten-year-old Honda Accord. Drew took Cassie to eat dinner at Dairy Delight, one of the two fast-food restaurants in Rockdale. He apologized for the less-than-high-class meal, explaining that his mom struggled to make ends meet for their family. Drew also let Cassie know that he worked after school and on the weekends at the country club in Mapleton and was saving for a car. It would be a while, but he hoped to buy one before Christmas so that he could drive himself to and from school during the second half of his senior year.

Truthfully, Cassie didn't care how much money his family had or whether he would save enough to buy a car. From the moment he introduced himself, she found herself very much attracted to Drew Cashwell. And that appeal grew with every new conversation. While she certainly thought Drew was cute, it was his sweet smile, engaging manner, and commitment to the Lord that made her want to spend more time with him.

So, they did. Until the end of the school year, they were together every weekend. They talked and texted every day. While there had been no official declaration or request by either, their status as boyfriend and girlfriend was cemented.

It was the only Friday in June that Drew did not have to work. He and Cassie made plans to spend the day together. They went swimming at the Rockdale Community Center that afternoon. Dinner was another fast-food meal at Dairy Delight. They watched a movie at her house that evening. It was the most time they'd spent together in one day, and they never grew bored or found their conversations lacking. It was, in both of their minds, their best date yet.

Drew thanked Mr. Ford for allowing him to come over, said goodbye, and walked outside to his car. Cassie accompanied Drew, just as she'd done many times before. As they held hands, he thanked her for a fun day. She smiled, told him to drive home safely, and wrapped her arms around his waist. He returned her hug, and they both held the embrace, longer than they ever had before. Drew felt his heart about to beat out of his chest as he debated attempting a first kiss with Cassie. Determined not to overthink this move, he eased his head back, leaned down and slowly brought his lips close to hers. Cassie instantly responded to his advance by tilting her head upwards and welcoming Drew's physical show of affection. For both, it was their first kiss together and their first kiss ever.

And it was wonderful.

Drew smiled the entire fifteen-minute drive back to Mapleton. He was head-over-heels in love, and he knew that Cassie was the one he would marry one day, someday. When they were out of high school, but maybe while they were still in college, if he could get a job while he went to school. Or, perhaps, they would marry after they graduated from college, but he really hoped they didn't have to wait that long. All he wanted was to be with Cassie every minute of the day. Leaving her house was painful. Neither wanted him to go, but he had to be home by 11:30 p.m., and the last thing he wanted was to lose the privilege of borrowing his mom's car and going to see Cassie.

These thoughts of the future flooded his mind as he drove. He arrived in Mapleton and took a right onto Main Street. His phone rested on the passenger seat beside him, and just after he made the turn, he heard the sound of a text notification. He looked over and saw that it was from Cassie. He couldn't wait to get home to read the message. He unlocked his phone and opened the text. His heart nearly leaped from his chest when he read the words she'd written:

> Thank you for a great time tonight!
> I think I've fallen in love with you!

He couldn't believe she was the first to put the "L" word out there. Sure, it wasn't exactly the phrase, "I love you," but it was close enough! He immediately began to text back, wanting her to know he felt the exact same way. At that moment, Drew Cashwell saw fireworks exploding all around him.

However, what he did not see was Mrs. Johnson's thirteen-year-old Golden Retriever slowly meandering across Main Street. Lucky was utterly blind, mostly deaf, and could not win a footrace against a turtle. He was notorious for wandering away from home, getting lost, and one of the neighbors having to guide him back to Mrs. Johnson's house. In that way, Lucky lived up to his name. People looked out for and helped take care of him.

He also lived up to his name this night. At the last possible minute, Drew glanced up and saw his headlights reflecting off Lucky's golden coat. Lucky, of course, made no attempt to either stop or accelerate his methodical, slow gait across Main Street. Drew jerked the steering wheel to the right, flew over the curb, the sidewalk, miraculously threaded the car between two maple trees, skidded through grass, a driveway, and finally came to a stop at the end of a flower bed. Fortunately, neither

Drew nor Lucky were injured. Unfortunately, Drew managed to destroy every single one of Judah Stephens' prized hydrangea bushes.

Invaluable was the word Judah continually used in describing the process of replacing his plants. He could put a price on wooden landscape timbers and the mulch—those items could easily be purchased from *The Garden Shop* in Mapleton. But the hydrangeas? That was another story. How could he find, purchase, and replant fully mature shrubs with blooms the exact color of his now demolished creation?

Of course, he couldn't. They were irreplaceable. Judah would've used the word *priceless*, except for the fact that Judah was determined to exact financial compensation from Drew Cashwell or his mom. He spent several hours on Saturday assessing the damage and calculating the cost of replacing the hydrangeas. Although they would not be exactly what he had, a specialty flower nursery in Atlanta carried mature shrubs. He called the store, spoke with a salesperson, and wrote down prices. Supplies and labor totaled just over $4,200. On Saturday evening, Judah called Drew's house and spoke with his mom about the cost to repair the damage.

Drew's mom didn't want to file a claim with insurance. She had opted for a very high deductible to save money. Plus, with Drew's ticket for texting while driving, their insurance rates would probably skyrocket anyway. A claim would only send it higher.

But she certainly didn't have that kind of cash on hand. Nor did Drew. He'd managed to save $1,200 from working at the Mapleton Country Club—money he was hoping to use for a future vehicle purchase. But, even with that amount saved, he was still $3,000 short. Drew called Mr. Stephens, offered the $1,200, and promised to get the rest to him as soon as possible.

However, a vague promise from a teenage boy wasn't enough for Judah Stephens. He demanded, no, he *deserved*, a legal means of ensuring that he would get paid. All his hard work was destroyed by the foolish actions of this kid who was texting while driving. There was no way he was going to trust the word of Drew Cashwell and simply hope for the best.

On Monday, Judah filed a claim in the Grant County Magistrate Court. As a county employee, he knew Judge Simmons well. He spoke with the judge on Tuesday, informed him of the situation, and demanded a quick hearing. The judge agreed, and two weeks later, Drew, Drew's mom, and Judah appeared before Judge Simmons.

Judah insisted he get his money as soon as possible. He deserved compensation for his losses, not to mention the time he'd invested in pricing the plants and materials. He should not have to wait months to collect.

With tears in his eyes, Drew begged Judge Simmons and Mr. Stephens for mercy. The only option they had to pay

Mr. Stephens would come from selling the Honda Accord. However, this action would place an enormous strain on both Drew and his mom. They needed reliable transportation to get to their jobs, to church, and to school.

Judah didn't care. This wasn't his fault. Drew caused this problem, so he and his mom would have to suffer the consequences of Drew's actions. The law was clear: the Cashwells were liable for the damages.

Finally, *reluctantly*, Judge Simmons ordered the sale of the car. A portion of the proceeds would go to pay the money owed to Judah Stephens. He rapped his gavel and closed the case.

Judah turned on his heels and left as Drew and his mom hugged and quietly wept in one another's arms.

Judah returned to work the next day with a smug satisfaction, celebrating his legal victory. *Justice has been served*, he thought to himself. Soon, he would be able to rebuild his horticultural masterpiece. Although he vigorously complained about the vehicular destruction of his prized garden, he secretly looked forward to immersing himself in the reconstructive process. He longed to see the workday end so he could race home and begin his labors.

While Judah obsessed over his landscaping ordeal, he was oblivious to the efforts of Mrs. Charlotte Johnson, the administrative assistant who worked just down the hall from his office. Six months earlier, Charlotte was contacted by an auditor from the state Attorney General's office. No, she was not in trouble, he assured her. However, there were some irregularities in Grant County's financial review from the previous year. At this point, the auditor simply needed information, as much as Charlotte could provide. As well, would Charlotte be willing to keep this matter quiet, at least until he could sort everything out?

Charlotte did as she was asked. Files, documents, receipts, reports, memos...anything and everything was scanned and emailed to the auditor's office in Atlanta. While concerned about where this investigation would lead, Charlotte knew she had done nothing wrong. Plus, the nice gentleman from the Attorney General's office assured her that this was just to clear up some confusion. Over a six-week period, Charlotte shared hundreds of files from her office.

It was the Friday afternoon after Judah's court victory. Around 2:00 p.m., Judah found himself staring at the clock, longing to leave the office and commence rebuilding his hydrangea garden. Although he normally enjoyed numbers and spreadsheets and data entry, at this moment he was quite bored with his job. Perhaps, he thought, he could take a sick day and leave early, but why use PTO when he only had a couple hours of this drudgery left?

At exactly 2:05 p.m. that afternoon, Judah's boredom suddenly ended as GBI investigators raided his office.

The lead agent presented a search warrant, and three other men seized Judah's computer and files. No, Judah was not under arrest. *Yet.* However, he was required to turn over his keys before these men escorted him out of the building. He would also need to report to the office for a meeting with his supervisor and state officials on the following Monday morning.

After a sleepless weekend, Judah drove to his office early that Monday. When he walked in the front door, agents met him with an arrest warrant. While one of the agents read him his Miranda Rights, Judah Stephens absolutely abided by his right to remain silent. He knew exactly why his hands were now bound by cuffs.

When Judah's attorney reviewed the case against him, he knew there was no hope for an acquittal. It required a large team of accountants to unravel the numbers. However, once they completed their assignment, the investigators had Judah dead to rights. Over a ten-year period, Judah had carefully siphoned off more than $800,000 from the county coffers for his personal use. He'd carefully coded the payments to different businesses, all seeming to be legitimate vendors used by the county: Hart's Landscaping Services, Smith and Sons Plumbers, Georgia Office Supplies, and Grant Lighting Company. All invoices contained thorough but completely fabricated explanations for the charges. In reality, there was no landscaping work done, no plumbing work completed; no office supplies purchased, and no new light fixtures installed. The so-called businesses had accounts with four different banks, each in a different neighboring county. Judah personally made the deposits with these financial institutions, then wrote checks to himself in amounts always under $5,000. Judah's plan was bullet-proof.

At least, that is what he believed.

His attorney contacted the D.A. and asked for a plea bargain. Judah would never survive a jury trial. The evidence was overwhelming.

The D.A. was ready to deal. He had an already crowded calendar and relished the idea of quickly resolving the case against Judah Stephens. He offered ten years of probation on two conditions: Judah pay back every dime he stole (with interest) within five years, and no attempts by Judah to secure future employment as an accountant or bookkeeper.

"This is a sweetheart deal," his attorney told Judah. "You need to accept and thank the good Lord for watching out for you."

Judah, his attorney, and the D.A. appeared in court the following Tuesday to present the terms of the plea bargain to the judge, who just happened to be Judge Simmons. He listened to the details of the agreement, staring intently at the D.A. as he spoke. When he finished outlining the conditions, Judge Simmons shook his head. "You've got to be kidding me," he said. "There is simply no way Judah Stephens will get off that easy for his crimes. He knowingly and brazenly stole nearly a million dollars from the citizens of this county. And based upon my previous dealings with Mr. Stephens,

I believe he understands that a price must be paid for wrongdoings."

"Therefore, here is the offer I'll present: 20 years in prison, with the possibility of parole after seven. And, every single dime, *with interest,* paid back to the county within the next four months. Even if it means selling that beautiful home on Main Street."

"Mr. Stephens, you can either accept the terms of that agreement or roll the dice with a jury trial. However, the members of the jury will be comprised of our county's tax-paying citizens, the very individuals from whom you stole. My guess is that just about any 12 of your neighbors would likely want to throw you under the jail."

Before his attorney could stop him from speaking, Judah practically shouted, "Your honor, please! Can't you show me a little mercy here? I have agreed to reimburse the county. I'll get a job, and you can garnish my wages. Just don't send me to prison and, for the love of God, don't make me sell my home!"

With a calm, firm voice, Judge Simmons said, "First of all, Mr. Stephens, *reimburse* is an incredibly poor word choice. Grant County *reimburses* employees for expenditures they incur while performing the duties of their job. You, on the other hand, blatantly robbed the county coffers for the last decade. You will not just *reimburse* the county for a legitimate business expense. You will *pay back* what you stole."

"Secondly, and more importantly, I would be far more inclined to extend some measure of mercy in this situation if I knew you to be a man of mercy. However, your recent actions made it abundantly clear that you are a harsh judge of other people's crimes. Therefore, Mr. Stephens, these are the best terms you will receive from me. Accept, or you can explain to a jury why you were justified in stealing from them over the last decade."

It took less than a minute for Judah's attorney to convince him to agree to Judge Simmons' terms. A sheriff's deputy then walked over to Judah, led him by the arm through a side door. He was then placed in the back of a police cruiser, and hauled to the county jail. Judah never again worked in his beautiful garden.

Gene Bridges was a member of Mapleton Country Club and the owner of Mapleton's only new car dealership: *Bridges Ford*. Over the previous year, while at the club, Mr. Bridges had quietly observed the work ethic of young Drew Cashwell. He noted that Drew would fix a problem or meet a need without being asked, an increasingly diminishing virtue among the younger generation, at least in the opinion of Mr. Bridges. Moreover, when Drew interacted with him or other individuals, he made eye contact, spoke respectfully, and always sought to fulfill any requests made of him by a club member. This young man was the kind of employee he wanted at his dealership.

Perhaps, one day, he would have the opportunity to present a job offer to Drew.

However, in the meantime, he knew Drew and his mom needed assistance. During a Saturday round of golf, Judge Simmons vented to Gene about the *Stephens v Cashwell* case. Sure, Drew should not have been texting while driving, but that pompous Judah Stephens acted like his hydrangea garden was the Mona Lisa. And now, the Cashwells would be forced to sell their only mode of transportation. It would be an incredible hardship on this single mom and her only son.

Gene knew he had to do something. Truthfully, he *wanted* to do something. He contacted the country club's general manager and asked for Drew's home number. Drew's mom answered the phone. Gene introduced himself, although she knew exactly who he was. He told her that he'd heard about their latest ordeal and wondered if she'd sold the Honda Accord yet. No, they had 30 days, and she was waiting as long as possible to sell. She needed transportation, and honestly didn't know what she would do once the car was gone. He told her he understood and asked if she and Drew would meet him at his dealership the next day. She agreed, secretly hoping he had a cheap car on his lot that he would be willing to finance over a lot of years.

The following morning, Drew and his mom sat in Mr. Bridges office at the dealership. After the initial pleasantries, Gene gave a high-level overview of vehicle depreciation and explained how some cars hold their value better than others. "Honda Accords," he said, "are at the top of the list. If you will sell me your car, I'll pay you top dollar for it."

He then made an extremely generous offer—one that would allow Drew to pay his debt and still have a significant sum of money left over.

"And" he continued, "we are running a special right now on our smaller SUV's. I can do 0% financing over seven years." Mr. Bridges then estimated a monthly payment, which was well within Mrs. Cashwell's budget.

"Before you go outside to look at cars, I'd like to make one more offer. I have a three-year-old used truck on my lot that just came in. It's in great shape and looks brand new. Drew, I've watched you at the club, and it's clear you have a strong work ethic. I have no doubt that you will be able to maintain employment, even after you graduate high school and go to college. I'd like to offer this truck to you at the trade-in value along with the same financing terms. We normally do not offer this kind of financing on used vehicles, but today I'd like to make an exception."

Drew and his mom were overjoyed. They walked outside, looked over the cars, and then walked back inside the dealership and signed the paperwork.

Drew shook hands with Mr. Bridges and thanked him for the hundredth time. He turned, hugged his mom, and told her he loved her.

Drew then opened the door to his used (but new to him) truck, sat in the driver's seat, and started the vehicle.

Then immediately drove to Rockdale.

QUESTIONS FOR DISCUSSION:

Ice-Breaker: Name a time in your life when you were shown incredible mercy.

1. What are some similarities between this story and the parable of Jesus? Differences?
2. Why did Judah feel so wronged by Drew's accident, yet see nothing wrong with his own actions?
3. Why are we so quick to judge others for their sin but excuse our own?
4. Read Luke 6:41-42. What do these verses tell us about judging others? Do these prohibit us from ever speaking to others about their sin? Why or why not?
5. Read Matthew 5:7. What did Jesus mean by this statement? How do we obtain mercy by showing mercy?
6. When is it easy for you to show mercy, and when is it the most difficult?
7. Can you name a time when you were shown mercy? How did that experience affect you?
8. Read Micah 6:8. What are some practical ways you can live out the commands of this verse?

CHAPTER 3
SAM'S TWO SONS
The Parable of the Two Sons

"What do you think? There was a man who had two sons. He went to the first and said, 'Son, go and work today in the vineyard.'

"'I will not,' he answered, but later he changed his mind and went.

"Then the father went to the other son and said the same thing. He answered, 'I will, sir,' but he did not go.

"Which of the two did what his father wanted?"

"The first," they answered.

Jesus said to them, "Truly I tell you, the tax collectors and the prostitutes are entering the kingdom of God ahead of you. For John came to you to show you the way of righteousness, and you did not believe him, but the tax collectors and the prostitutes did. And even after you saw this, you did not repent and believe him.

Matthew 21:28-32

A Few Comments...

Jesus told this parable just days before his crucifixion. Although the crowds shouted, "Hosanna, blessed is he who comes in the name of the Lord," as Jesus rode a donkey into Jerusalem, his life was on a trajectory that would eventually lead him to the cross. Shortly after entering the city, Jesus overturned the tables of the money changers and the benches of those selling doves. This action interrupted a significant financial operation of the temple authorities. Suddenly, those who had previously tolerated the unorthodox ministry of Jesus now found their patience wearing thin.

Soon afterwards, Jesus told this parable, aimed directly at the hypocrisy of the religious leaders. One son refuses the father's request to work but ultimately decides to do what his father asked. The other son readily agrees to work in the vineyard but plays hooky instead.

Every dad and mom can identify with this scenario. The obedience comes not from agreeing to follow a parent's instructions but from actually doing what was asked. The religious leaders knew this truth, and acknowledged as much when Jesus asked, "Which of the two did what his father wanted?"

Jesus then turned their attention to John the Baptist. Israel's religious establishment made a grand show of their commitment, but they refused to repent and follow the teachings of John. However, those who were religious outcasts—the prostitutes, tax-collectors, and sinners—they repented, were baptized, and followed John's instructions.

It's easy to see why, a few days later, the religious leaders were so intent on having Jesus crucified. Through his actions and words, Jesus quickly made some powerful enemies.

Let's turn our attention to a modern story that highlights this same truth.

SAM'S TWO SONS

The rumors swirled among the gathered crowd at the All-American Cafe. Customers routinely checked their phones for texts with the latest information. Various accounts, mostly conjecture, were offered by the patrons. The stories were heard, digested, analyzed, and debated. Unsubstantiated details were shared and spread throughout the crowded restaurant on this September morning.

Only two things were known for sure. First, Sam Underwood was, by a mile, the best auto mechanic in all of Grant County. Sam's Auto Shop sat half a block from Main Street, just behind The Dollar Mart. Sam was a Mapleton native who did a four-year stint in the Army after graduating high school. While in the service, he learned how to repair Jeeps and transport vehicles. He was a quick learner and naturally knew his way around an engine. A customer once told Sam he was "Michelangelo with a torque wrench." Sam smiled and thanked the customer, although he wasn't exactly sure which Major League Baseball team Michael Angelo played for.

Sam opened the shop when he was only 23 years old, using the money he'd saved while in the Army and a small loan from First National Bank of Grant County. That same year, Sam married his high school sweetheart, a relationship that somehow had managed to survive his tour of duty. Sadly, when she was only 43, Sam's wife passed away from cancer. She was his one and only love, and Sam swore he would never marry again.

Now, at 60 years of age, Sam was entirely devoted to his auto garage. He'd worked on the vehicles of nearly every citizen of Mapleton. It was a well-established fact that Sam only fixed what needed to be fixed, never overcharged for parts or services, and finished the job on schedule. If he was overrun with cars, he would tell a customer that it would be a week or two before he could get to it. They could either wait or go to another mechanic. Virtually all chose to wait.

The second known certainty was that whatever happened in his shop on that morning was tragic. Sam was injured, and badly. Some kind of accident occurred while he was working in his garage. At this point, the information had to be pieced together from several different sources. The only consistent account was that an ambulance took Sam to Grant County Hospital, and from there, he was life-flighted to Banks Memorial in Atlanta.

Other rumors—that he was on life-support, that he died during the flight, that he was in surgery and not expected to survive—were unverified and contradicted one another. Numerous calls were made, and texts sent, trying to get more information. Every new detail was instantly lapped up and digested by the curious crowd.

A group of men stood outside the cafe, in a circle, all smoking cigarettes and bemoaning the fact that they were no longer allowed to smoke inside the restaurant. More conjecturing and prognosticating happened as smoke rings billowed above the small gathering. Chief among the concerns was the future of Sam's garage. Not only was Sam the best mechanic in town, but he was also the only one trusted by these men. Each, it seemed, had a story to tell about the mechanical problems they'd faced over the years and how Sam was able to diagnose and repair issues at a reasonable cost. All nodded their heads in agreement when one of the gentlemen said, "I just don't know where I'll take my truck if Sam isn't around."

A few minutes later, a waitress opened the front door, stuck her head out, and told the men to come inside. "We just got a call from Sammy. You boys need to hear this." They quickly threw their cigarettes down, ground them into the pavement, and filed back into the diner. Tommy McClendon, the owner, had just gotten everyone's attention and told them that he'd talked with Sam's oldest son.

"Sammy is on the way to Banks Memorial right now. Sam is stable, but he lost a lot of blood. Sammy said he would call me back once he got to the hospital and figured out exactly what was going on."

"Did he say what happened, Tommy?"

"Apparently, the locking mechanism on the car lift snapped. Sam was underneath the vehicle when he heard the lock break. The car tilted and started falling. He managed to move quickly enough to get out from under it, but the bumper caught his leg on the way down. Cut an artery and he bled a lot. Sounds like he's lucky to be alive."

Samuel Underwood, Jr.—"Sammy" to all of his family and friends—was the eldest son of Sam. Sammy lived in Mapleton, where he worked as a Certified Public Accountant. Sammy graduated with honors from Mapleton High School, majored in accounting at the University of Georgia, and returned to his hometown after marrying a girl he met during his sophomore year at UGA. He immediately joined the Mapleton Country Club, the Chamber of Commerce, and the Rotary Club. Sammy was a model son to his parents, a model student while in school, and later a model citizen of the community.

Sam's younger son, John, lived in Atlanta. He was the polar opposite of his big brother. John was often described as a lost cause. Sometimes as hopeless. He was brilliant, but lazy. John scored a 1480 on his SAT, but his high school GPA was an abysmal 2.6. Even so, the admissions counselor at the University of Georgia recommended taking a chance on John. He was accepted but completely wasted his first semester. When Sam learned that John had managed to procure two Cs and three Fs that fall, he refused to pay another dime for his youngest son's education, or lack thereof.

John immediately moved back home and went to work in his dad's garage, cleaning up and doing whatever menial tasks Sam could find for his son. Truthfully, both hated the arrangement. Sam felt like it was more work on him to keep John busy, but there was no way he would allow his youngest son to stay home and do nothing. After only a couple of weeks, however, the tension became unbearable. The shouting match between Sam and John happened on a Friday afternoon and resulted in John leaving the garage, going home, packing a few of his belongings, and crashing at a friend's house for a week.

Eventually, John made his way to Atlanta. A friend from college had a buddy who lived there and worked for—of all businesses—an auto garage. John was offered a job. He lived with this friend for a couple of weeks until he managed to squirrel enough money away to rent a dump of an apartment. He didn't care if it was hardly a step above a rat-infested hovel. It was his place, and he could do whatever he wanted. And *whatever* typically included alcohol, drugs, or a combination of the two. He made enough money to pay his bills, barely, and had a little left over to support his debauchery. John worked during the days and spent his evenings and weekends with friends who possessed his same passion to escape reality using mind-altering substances.

Although estranged from his father, John discovered during this time that he had inherited Sam's knack for mechanical repairs. He'd picked up a lot of knowledge as a child and teenager just by hanging around his dad's shop, but always seemed disinterested or lazy. However, at his new place of employment, his automotive genius was evident. John was a quick study and, after only a few months of working in the garage, could handle most repair jobs without assistance. Even when he was hungover from a night filled with alcohol or drugs, he could diagnose and repair automotive issues better than anyone else in the shop.

Sammy sat in the ICU of Banks Memorial with his father. Tubes and wires ran from every part of Sam's body. The doctor who met with Sam explained that the injury sustained in the garage had cut into Sam's femoral artery and that he'd lost a lot of blood.

"We managed to give him four units," the doctor said, "and he has stabilized as a result. However, the sudden blood loss caused AKI, or an Acute Kidney Injury, in both of Sam's kidneys. We want to give it a little more time, but we fear he may be in renal failure. We can do dialysis, but this is not a permanent solution. He needs a transplant, and, in my experience, family members are often the best candidates to serve as donors."

"What are you saying, doc?"

"I'm saying that our next step is to run some tests on you and any other close family members who are willing to be considered as a donor. Do you have any brothers or sisters you can contact? Or does your father have brothers or sisters who are healthy enough for surgery? The tests won't take long, and we can determine who is and who is not viable."

"Dad had one older sister. She died of a heart attack four years ago. He has one other son, my younger brother. I'll get in contact with him and relay what you've told me."

"That's good. Most likely one or both of you will be a fit. And in our experience, a kidney from an immediate family member is far less likely to be rejected and will continue functioning twice as long as kidneys from non-family members. Although we can't know for sure, a kidney from you or your brother might very well last your father for the rest of his life."

"Thanks for the information, Doc. I'll let you know when my brother arrives."

"You've got to be kidding me!" John practically shouted through the phone to Sammy. "Ain't no way I'm giving up a kidney! What if my other one fails some day? There's a reason people were born with two kidneys, Sammy! Everybody needs a backup. With all the alcohol I've consumed in my life, I'm sure one of mine is about to shut down anyway."

"I think alcohol ruins your liver, not your kidneys."

"Really? How many livers do we have?"

"Just one."

"Guess I'm doomed."

"Look, John. You need to come up here and see Dad anyway. At this point all they will do is a quick blood test. I think they may do more tests later, but this is the first step to determine if you're even a viable match. If you are, then you can make the decision about whether to give up one of your kidneys. If not, then you did all you can do, and that'll be it.

"I don't know, Sammy. I just don't know if I can do it."

"You don't have to decide now. Come to Banks Memorial to visit with Dad, and you can figure out what you're going to do once you get here."

Sammy and John entered the ICU room and stared at their father, almost in disbelief over his weakened state. Sam was always the one who exuded strength and confidence in every situation. They hardly ever saw their father lying down, doing nothing, not busy with work or some household project. They often joked that he was the Energizer Bunny, always on the go and never taking time to rest and relax.

Now, however, the situation was much different. Sam looked pale and weak. An oxygen tube hung from his nose and wires attached to seemingly every square inch of his chest. Sam was awake, but his eyes betrayed the fact that he wasn't his normal, mentally sharp self. The accident and resulting injuries to his body stole Sam's usual vigor and vitality.

Sammy walked over to Sam and stood beside him, looking stoically at his father. John nervously paced the small area in the room, from the end of the bed to the wall and back.

"Dad, how are you feeling?" Sammy's question interrupted the constant, methodical beeps of the monitors and the whir of the oxygen machine.

"Okay," Sam mumbled, almost in a whisper. "Think I've had better days."

"Dad, you'll be fine. Your leg will heal, and after you get a new kidney, you'll make a full recovery."

"Sounds good," Sam sleepily mumbled. "Can you run over to Walmart and buy me a kidney?"

Sammy smiled. "Dad, John and I are getting tested. One of us will surely be a donor match for you."

"*Mmmh.*" John continued his pacing as he snorted. "*Mmmh. Mmmh. Mmmh.* I just don't know."

"What don't you know?" Sammy asked, raising his voice well above a hushed whisper.

"I can't just give up one of my kidneys! I mean, that's major surgery. How long will I have to be out of work? I don't have a cushy job like you, Sammy, where I can sit all day. If I don't work, I don't get paid, and I can't really put in a new transmission if I'm bleeding out of my side. I just don't know."

Sammy walked over to John, grabbed him by the arm,

and sternly whispered, "You're really going to say all this in front of Dad?!? Just shut up, why don't you? If you don't want to give up a kidney, then fine. But can you at least be a more sensitive to his feelings?"

John grunted, jerked his arm away from Sammy, and left the room. Sammy turned and walked back to the side of his father's bed. Sam was groggy but heard and understood every word spoken between his two sons. Sammy looked apologetically at his father, as if to say, "I'm sorry you had to hear that." Sam reached over and placed his hand on top of Sammy's. He looked up at his oldest son and, in a scratchy whisper, said, "Everything's going to be okay."

Sammy sat in a small room located on the fourth floor of the hospital, nervously tapping his feet while waiting for the phlebotomist. According to the medical staff, the blood test was the first step to determine if he was a viable donor. There were other tests, sure, but they were more extensive and expensive. The blood work would not guarantee that he was a match, but it could rule him out. If it did, they would need to search for other possible donors.

"Samuel Underwood?" the woman asked as she entered the room, looking down at a clipboard holding several sheets of paper.

"Uh, yes, that's right. I go by Sammy."

"And what is your date of birth?"

Sammy looked at the hospital badge clipped to her scrubs. Darlene something or other was her name. He'd noticed at this hospital the badges all had the first names in large print and the staff's last names in smaller print underneath. I guess it was an effort to create a friendlier, more familial environment.

"Darlene. I guess it's okay if I call you Darlene, right? Look, I need your help. There is no reason for you to draw blood. I can't do this thing. I'm not giving up a kidney, but I can't bear the thought of my dad or others knowing this. I need you or whoever to just say that I'm not a viable donor, but you can't tell anyone that I didn't want to give up a kidney. I mean, with HIPPA, you guys are sworn to secrecy, aren't you?"

"Yes, but HIPPA doesn't mean we have to lie. We can't say you're not a viable donor if we don't know whether you're a viable donor. Look, it's your kidney and your choice, Mr. Underwood, but I cannot fabricate a story."

"If you do not draw my blood, can you honestly say that you were unable to determine if I am a viable donor? It would just break my dad's heart if he thought I wasn't willing to do this thing. He's struggling enough right now as it is. I don't want him to end up worse off by getting this devastating news."

Darlene stared at Sammy, thinking about his question and wondering exactly how to answer. After a few seconds, she broke the silence and responded. "I guess

I could say that. I wouldn't say I particularly like that answer, though. It's the truth, but not the whole truth. However, I certainly don't want to do anything to upset your dad. So, yeah, I guess I can just tell him that we weren't able to know for sure if you'd be a match."

"What do you mean they couldn't determine if you're a viable donor?" John practically shouted at his older brother. "That doesn't make any sense. Tell them to run the test again!"

Sammy and John sat in chairs across from one another in the family waiting room of the ICU section. John was a basket of emotions while his older brother spoke in a calm, steady voice.

"It's not that simple, John. These tests are expensive. Insurance won't pay for further testing at this point. They will only cover the initial blood tests for other possible donors. If none come forward, then Dad will just go on the national list for a kidney."

"How long will it take him to get a kidney that way?"

"Not sure. It could be a long time. Just depends on donors out there, who else needs a kidney, and whether the donor is a match to Dad. The other issue is that a kidney from a non-family member typically doesn't last as long. According to the doctor, a kidney from a close relative would most likely serve him the rest of his life.

A kidney from a random donor would probably end up failing at some point."

"Dang, Sammy. You sure know how to pile the guilt on, don't you?"

"John, I'm just giving you the facts. It's your life. It's your kidney. Don't get tested if you don't want."

"But if I don't, you're saying it might not end well for Dad?"

"I'm not saying anything. I just don't know."

"Man, Sammy. I mean, you're the brother who always does exactly what is right. You're the one Dad and everyone else can count on. I'm the screw-up. Everybody looks at me and thinks I only care about myself. And, you know, there are times that has certainly been the case. But I do love Dad. Even with all our fights, I love him. We haven't always seen eye to eye, but that's mainly because I'm the idiot, not Dad. I sure don't want to give up a kidney, but I can't stand the thought of not helping the old man."

John paused, hung his head and studied his shoes for a few seconds, then let out an exasperated sigh. *"Fine.* Tell me where to go to get that blood test. If I'm a match, I'll do it. I'll give up my kidney. If I'm not, then we'll just have to hope for the best."

It was three months later, on a Friday afternoon, that Sam, Sammy, and John found themselves sitting in

Sam's office at the garage. This was the first time the three had been in the same room since the surgeries and Sam's release from the hospital. John had requested the afternoon off, and his boss was more than willing to grant it. John was his most valuable employee, and he wanted to keep him happily employed. John left early enough to avoid the Atlanta rush-hour traffic and rolled into Mapleton just after one o'clock.

Sammy, as the owner of his CPA firm, told his assistant that he was leaving the office early and would be out the rest of the afternoon. Sammy was the one who had asked for this meeting with his dad to discuss his path forward after the kidney transplant—what he could eat and not eat, his medications, his future appointments, and, most importantly, the firm instructions on what he should and should not do at the shop. Truthfully, Sammy had no intention of inviting John. It was Sam who called John and asked him to come that afternoon. As Sammy went through his spiel, John offered no commentary or advice. He was an observer, not exactly sure why his father wanted him here.

"Listen, Sammy, I hear you," Sam said. "Thank you for handling all of this, and just know that I appreciate all you've done. And I promise you I will be careful. I won't work alone on a Saturday morning, and I'll let these younger mechanics do the heavy lifting."

"Okay, Dad. Look, I've got to get to a tee time at the club. I'm sure I'll see you at some point this weekend. John, good to see you as well. Look, come by the house sometime. The kids would love to see 'Fun Uncle John.' They always light up when you're around."

John nodded and offered a non-committal, "Sure. I'd like that."

"Thanks again for all you've done," Sam said to his oldest son. "Have a great weekend."

Sam then turned to John. "Can you stay just a little while longer?"

After Sammy walked out, Sam asked his youngest son. "How are you feeling?"

"Umm, fine. I'm pretty much back to doing everything at work that I did before."

"John, I know you and I have had our differences in the past, and I have been hard on you sometimes. And I know you were really anxious about giving up your kidney. But, at the end of the day, you came through for me, and I am forever grateful. I love you, son."

"I love you, too, Dad. Look, I know I sort of flipped out in your hospital room that day when Sammy started talking about one of us donating a kidney. It just threw me. Big time. And I wasn't sure what all was involved and thought it would be a much harder deal. But, when it turned out that Sammy wasn't a viable donor, I knew I needed to step in. It hasn't been nearly as much of an ordeal as I thought. I guess, really, I'm sort of glad that Sammy couldn't be a donor. It meant that I could be the one to help this time."

Sam thought long and hard about how to respond to John. During his recovery, a nurse "accidentally" left a clipboard next to Sam's hospital bed. On the clipboard were the nurse's notes about Sammy's unwillingness to have his blood drawn. She had witnessed the interaction between the two brothers and their father and wanted so badly for Sam to know the truth. However, she understood her professional obligation of confidentiality. She would not say a word to Sam or anyone else about what she knew.

But everyone makes small mistakes, right? It's not unusual at all for a doctor or nurse to set something on a table, forget about it, and only later realize that said item had been left behind. Thirty minutes after checking on Sam, she returned to his room and apologized for leaving her clipboard on the table next to his hospital bed. She smiled at this man who had quickly become one of her favorite patients, winked, and left the room.

Sam had read it all.

But there was no reason to reveal what he knew to John. It would only cause a rift between his two sons—brothers who rarely saw eye-to-eye on much of anything anyway.

"I'm glad too, John. You're a good son. So is Sammy. I know both of you love me."

But Sam knew which son really loved him the most.

QUESTIONS FOR DISCUSSION:

Ice-Breaker: Have you ever made a commitment, but later realized you didn't want to follow through with it? What did you do?

1. What are some similarities between this story and the parable of Jesus? Differences?
2. As you were introduced to the characters in the story, which son did you think would come to the aid of Sam?
3. Which son really loved Sam, and which son just loved appearing to be the good son?
4. Read Matthew 21:45-46. When Jesus told the parable of the two sons, who were his listeners? Why were they so offended by his words?
5. How can we keep an appearance of religion but have a heart that isn't right with God?
6. How were tax-collectors and sinners viewed in that society? How were they like the first son in the parable?
7. The clear point of this parable is that actions are more important than empty promises. How does this apply to our relationship with God?
8. Read Isaiah 29:13. What does this verse say about our speech and actions?
9. Read Matthew 6:1-4. What are ways we act like the hypocrites in our giving? What are we instructed to do in our giving?

10. Read Matthew 6:5-6. What are ways we can act like the hypocrites in our praying? What are we instructed to do in our praying?
11. Read Matthew 6:16-18. What are ways we can act like the hypocrites in our fasting? What are we instructed to do when we fast? Why is this so important?

CHAPTER 4
PENNY'S PLEAS
The Parable of the Persistent Widow

Then Jesus told his disciples a parable to show them that they should always pray and not give up. He said: "In a certain town there was a judge who neither feared God nor cared what people thought. And there was a widow in that town who kept coming to him with the plea, 'Grant me justice against my adversary.'

"For some time he refused. But finally he said to himself, 'Even though I don't fear God or care what people think, yet because this widow keeps bothering me, I will see that she gets justice, so that she won't eventually come and attack me!'"

And the Lord said, "Listen to what the unjust judge says. And will not God bring about justice for his chosen ones, who cry out to him day and night? Will he keep putting them off? I tell you, he will see that they get justice, and quickly. However, when the Son of Man comes, will he find faith on the earth?"

Luke 18:1-8

A Few Comments...

The first step in analyzing a parable is to understand who the various characters represent. In this story, it is easy to identify the link with two of the individuals. The first is a widow. In that day, widows were virtually powerless. They typically had little money and almost always no power or authority. Jesus is clear that this widow represents us.

"Wait," you may say. "I have money and power. And I'm an influential person in my community!"

While that may be the case, can your wealth and authority solve every problem you face? Will your money fix a disobedient child, cure a cancer diagnosis, or heal a broken marriage? More importantly, can your status solve your sin problem and gain you entrance into heaven?

We are all like the widow, poor and dependent on someone else for assistance.

Enter character number two, the antagonist. This villain represents some problem we face. Jesus gave almost no details about the woman's adversary; however, it's clear that this individual harmed this widow in some way. An injustice has been committed against her, and she both desires and deserves to have this situation resolved.

But, in Jesus' day, the Romans often decided these cases. In this parable, the judge is described as "godless." He will happily give her justice if she will just slip him a bribe. Yet, she has no money. She has no power. There is no way for her to strong-arm her way to justice.

However, she *does* have persistence. She goes to the judge, day after day, pleading her case. She wears him down to the point that he finally agrees to her request.

Now, this is where the parable gets tricky. First, are we to surmise from this story that God is like this unjust, corrupt judge? Of course not. This is what is called a "study in contrasts." Jesus points out that if a godless, no-good judge will eventually answer a request, how much more will our Heavenly Father grant us what we ask when we pray?

This leads us to the second sticking point of this parable. Did Jesus mean that if we bug God, we will get what we want? If we pray about a need often enough, we will eventually have that request answered?

Not exactly. The point of this parable is to encourage us to be men and women of prayer. A life marked by persistent prayer is key to seeing the Lord do great things. Our requests may not be answered in the fashion we desire, but that doesn't mean our prayers are in vain. Keep praying. Continue to spend time with the Lord. Don't give up, and you'll see God answer in ways you could not have expected.

Now, let's see how Penny's persistence allowed her to get justice.

PENNY'S PLEAS

Penelope Rogers typically worked the second shift at the All-American Cafe. Although most waiters and waitresses wanted the earlier slots, Penny enjoyed the later hours. Truthfully, she was something of a night-owl, hated getting up early, and loved her slow, lazy mornings. She usually woke around 9:00 a.m., stayed in bed until 10:00 a.m., reading a book or checking messages on her phone, then finally emerged from her soft covers to eat breakfast and prepare for her day. She would then run errands, clean up around the house, and change into her uniform to be at the restaurant by 2:00 p.m. and work until 10:00 p.m.

Fifteen years earlier, Penny and her husband, Ben, moved to Mapleton from Cobb County, Georgia. Ben worked for MaxiTire, a heavy equipment tire manufacturer. He sold tires to virtually any business utilizing tractors, forklifts, cranes, bulldozers, or other heavy machinery. His territory covered the southern half of Georgia—from south of Atlanta to Valdosta—and he was rarely in the office. He believed face-to-face meetings and handshakes were far more effective than emails and phone calls. His customers trusted Ben, as did his employer. Ben had the freedom to work his schedule as he saw fit.

Which is why, when their youngest son graduated from high school to attend Mercer University in Macon,

Georgia, Ben and Penny made plans to move from their home in Atlanta. For years, they'd discussed purchasing a stately old home in a small town. One that sat on a main street lined with trees. Perhaps elm trees. Or towering oaks. A place where they could walk to the grocery store or to a local park. A town where they felt the freedom to drop in on their neighbors, maybe borrow a cup of sugar, and catch up on the latest gossip. They wanted a community where they could show up at a Fourth of July celebration and know most people in attendance.

They gave their real estate agent the names of several small towns, all located in Middle and South Georgia. When their realtor emailed them the information for 130 Main Street in Mapleton, they knew they'd found their new home.

The listing described it as a grand, four-over-four, brick Federal-style home constructed in 1928 and completed just one year before the Great Depression swept across the nation. Four bedrooms upstairs rested on top of a kitchen, dining room, library, and den. A magnificent hallway with a soaring staircase split the house in half. In the 1950s, the small kitchen was expanded to the rear of the home, with a laundry room and garage added. In 1970, a young local attorney and his wife purchased the home and added a screened-in porch and swimming pool. In 1995, that same attorney and a new wife completely renovated the home with new cabinets, fixtures, new plumbing, new wiring, and a new roof. The bones of the house were sturdy and solid. The modern updates gave it a practical livability.

PENNY'S PLEAS

It was the perfect house.

Six months after moving to Mapleton, Ben finally saw a doctor about his nagging, persistent cough. At forty-one years old, he was diagnosed with stage-4 lung cancer. Ben had smoked cigarettes most of his adult life. He wanted to give up the habit, but it helped pass the time as he traveled all over the state to meet with customers. The oncologist told Ben and Penny that chemo and radiation could extend his life by nine months, perhaps. Or, they could simply enjoy the remaining time they had and forgo the grueling side effects of the cancer treatment. They chose the latter option.

Two days before Penny's fortieth birthday, Ben passed away. She never expected—no one does—to become a widow at such an early age. Moreover, she found herself living alone in a still-unfamiliar town. Penny considered moving back to Cobb County, except that would put her farther away from her son. And she *really* loved the house that she and Ben had found together in Mapleton. Although they had lived there for less than a year, it was the first house that had genuinely felt like home for both. Plus, even a small home in Cobb County would be expensive. Ben and Penny had made a large down payment on this home, meaning she had a manageable mortgage payment. Within a week after Ben's funeral, Penny had made up her mind.

She was staying in Mapleton.

Initially, Penny lived off the funds received from the life insurance policy carried on Ben by his employer. It gave her time to grieve, close her husband's accounts, decide which of his personal items to keep and which to give away, and finish the house projects she and Ben had started before his diagnosis.

Eighteen months after his death, though, Penny knew she would need to find employment. This would not be easy. Penny and Ben met during her first year at West Georgia College. He was starting his senior year. They both quickly fell head-over-heels in love. It was less than a year later when Penny discovered she was pregnant. She and Ben considered all their options and concluded that they needed to get married, find an apartment, let Ben secure a job, and Penny would be a stay-at-home mom, at least initially. Once life had settled down, she would eventually return to school and obtain her degree.

But, *eventually* never happened. Ben found employment with MaxiTire, initially fulfilling client orders and later finding his true calling as a salesman. When their son entered middle school, Penny accepted a job working as a secretary at his school. She was able to earn a little extra income for the family yet remain available after school and on breaks.

Then, her son graduated, and she resigned from her position so that she and Ben could move to Mapleton. Their plan was for her to find a job, perhaps part-time, once they had settled into their new home and completed the hundreds of items on their to-do list. Of course, Ben's cancer changed all those plans.

Now, she found herself needing employment.

Not being a Mapleton native, Penny wasn't sure where to begin. Her sweet, elderly neighbor, Mrs. Johnson, had been one of the few to visit after Ben's death. Mrs. Johnson always brought food whenever she called on Penny, always invited Penny to come to worship with her at First Baptist, always asked how she could pray for Penny, and always asked if there was anything she could do for her.

On one visit, Penny replied, "Yes, actually, there is. I need a job. I don't have a college degree, which I know limits my options. I was a secretary at a middle school in Cobb County for seven years, but I don't have any other experience. Do you know of anything that is available?"

"Actually, I do. There is a young man named Tommy McClendon in our church. He is a wonderful Christian man with a sweet, sweet family. He owns the All-American Cafe, which I'm sure you've visited at some point during your time here in Mapleton. He needs servers at his place. Now, I know it doesn't sound all that glamorous being a waitress, but I promise you, there is no better employer than Tommy. He will treat you well, pay you fairly, give you time off when you need it, and, most importantly, his is the only restaurant in town closed on Sundays. Which means you'll never have to work on Sundays and can attend church with me."

Penny wasn't sure about waitressing, but she had grown to trust Mrs. Johnson's wisdom and opinions. She figured it was at least worth a conversation with Tommy McClendon.

That is how Penny ended up working as a waitress at the All-American Cafe.

Dwayne Sheffield was widely considered the sleaziest attorney ever to grace the courtrooms of Mapleton. Dwayne was notorious for filing frivolous lawsuits in the hopes of securing a financial settlement, never intending for the baseless cases to go to trial. He once famously sued the Graco Tool Company on behalf of a client who shot himself in the leg with a framing nailer. The client admitted that he thought the gun was out of nails and, just to be sure, placed it against his leg and fired. Obviously, he was mistaken, and there was, indeed, one more nail in the gun.

Dwayne claimed that Graco should have placed a warning on the nail gun itself, not just in the instructions (which no one ever reads). Moreover, he argued that the company was negligent in the design of its nailers because they fired when placed against the soft material of blue jeans and not just hard surfaces. Although frivolous and absurd, Graco realized their legal fees could easily skyrocket if the case went to trial. They settled for $50,000, a third of which lined the pockets of Mr. Sheffield.

Dwayne's moral deficiencies extended beyond his legal practice. His multiple affairs led to three failed marriages, all of which cost him significant amounts of the wealth he'd acquired through his dubious legal career. The third divorce happened when Dwayne was 64, and wife number three retained an attorney just as unscrupulous and vicious as her soon-to-be ex-husband. The financial settlement meant he was forced to sell his home, the one he'd lived in for over thirty years, and through his three marriages.

The home, located at 130 Main Street, sold to a couple from Cobb County, Georgia. It was just after the turn of the millennium and during a brief decline in the housing market. He begrudgingly signed the paperwork, selling the house at 20% less than he believed it was worth. Only a few years earlier, he and his then-wife had spent well over six figures on a major renovation of the home. Sadly, this money wasn't recouped in the sale. Even if it had, he consoled himself, most of it would end up in his now ex-wife's bank account. So, he practically gave away his home and moved into an apartment complex located on the north side of Mapleton.

Dwayne's son, Jim, was born to him and his first wife just a year after they purchased and moved into the home on Main Street. Jim spent the entirety of his childhood and teenage years in that house. Even though there were difficult times—his parents' divorce, his mom moving to Texas just to get far away from his father, his father's second marriage and that divorce—Jim held fond memories of the home. He and his friends spent hours hanging out on the screen porch and swimming in the pool. While in high school, his house became the gathering place for many of his classmates. His father was rarely around and did a poor job monitoring the activities of Jim and his friends. If someone managed to secure alcohol, Jim's home was the place where it could be consumed. Jim remembered those years as the best time of his life.

After graduating from high school, Jim enrolled at the University of Alabama. It was where his father had attended, and although Jim's high school grades were less than stellar, Dwayne's substantial monetary contributions to the school helped Jim receive a letter of acceptance.

However, during his first semester, Jim decided that school was only fun if one didn't attend class. That December, he was politely invited to leave the school and pursue other endeavors. He did and made his way to Colorado, where he found work at a ski resort in the winter and as a fishing guide during the summer months. Jim never married. He made enough money to afford a place to rent, food, clothes, and plenty of beer and liquor. He spent more than two decades drifting through life.

On the morning of his fortieth birthday, he received a call from Grant County Sheriff Ralph Peterman, who also happened to be one of Jim's best friends in high school. "Jim, I'm sorry to tell you this, but your father was found dead in his home this morning. Maybe a stroke or perhaps a heart attack. Not sure."

Jim spent his entire birthday driving, headed back to Mapleton.

Fortunately for Jim and his older sister, their father had remained unmarried after his third divorce. Additionally, he'd managed to rebuild a good portion of his wealth in his later years. Once everything was dispersed, Jim's share of the inheritance was a little more than $1,000,000. It was far more money than Jim had ever possessed in his life. It probably wasn't enough to keep him from ever having to work again, but it would enable him to make an offer on the one thing in Mapleton he *really* wanted—130 Main Street. He'd heard from his sheriff friend that a widow currently lived in his childhood home. She and her now-deceased husband purchased the house from his father in the aftermath of divorce number three. According to Ralph, she wasn't particularly wealthy. In fact, she worked as a waitress for Tommy McClendon, a former classmate of theirs. "Yeah," Ralph said, "I would assume she would be open to an offer. It doesn't hurt to ask."

Which is exactly what Jim intended to do. It was a Friday evening when he strolled through the front doors of the All-American Cafe. He noticed Tommy standing behind the counter, dutifully folding silverware into napkins. He walked over and greeted him like they were long-lost friends. Truthfully, Tommy and Jim never spent much time together in high school. Still, Tommy responded cordially, expressed his condolences over the passing of Jim's dad, and asked if there was anything he could do for Jim. "Yes," Jim replied. "You've got a waitress named Penny who lives in my old house. Can you tell me which section is hers? I'd like the chance to talk to her and ask her a few questions about the place."

Tommy directed Jim to a booth and told him Penny would be there shortly. A few minutes later, she greeted Jim with, "So, I hear you grew up in my house?"

"Well, yes," he said with a chuckle. "Except, I'd like to think of it as you now live in *my* house."

"Unfortunately for you, that's not what the deed says."

"Details, details," he replied with a grin. "Look, I just arrived back in town. My father—the one you bought the house from—recently passed away. I've been gone a long time, and I'm looking to settle back here where I grew up. And to be honest with you, I just can't imagine living here in my hometown anywhere besides that house. It was all I ever knew during my years in this town."

"So," Jim said as he leaned back in his booth, "I'd like to make you an offer. One that I really hope you'll consider."

"I'll be happy to consider it," she replied, "but I can almost guarantee you that the answer will be 'no.' My husband and I bought that house together. It was supposed to be our last home purchase. So, feel free to make your offer, but I would hate to waste your time."

Jim then grabbed a napkin from the container at the end of the table and quickly scribbled out a number. He then turned the napkin so Penny could clearly see the figure—an amount that was a very fair price for the house. However, she wasn't interested, and just shook her head and said, "I really hate to waste your time. Can I get you anything to eat?"

Jim turned the napkin, crossed through that his original offer, wrote another, significantly higher number below it and slid it across the table. This time, it gave Penny pause, knowing that she could walk away from the home with a considerable amount of cash in hand. But, still, she did not want to move. She said nothing and slid the napkin back to Jim.

He let out an exasperated huff, crossed through the second offer, and wrote a third figure below it. He then turned the napkin toward Penny and said, "Final offer. Take it or leave it." This number was 50% more than the original offer, and really did make Penny think about the freedom she would gain from this kind of money. Perhaps she could work a lot less and spend more time with her son, daughter-in-law, and new grandchild. And maybe travel some. Possibly upgrade her car and her wardrobe.

Yet, she knew she didn't want to leave the house. It was her connection with Ben, and it meant too much to her. She shook her head and said, "Are you sure there's nothing I can get for you to eat?"

Jim's cheeks turned red as a scowl formed on his face. He grunted and replied gruffly, "No, I think I've lost my appetite." He grabbed his jacket from the booth and stormed out of the All-American Cafe.

It was the following Tuesday morning when Penny awoke and noticed a strange, foul smell in her house. She exited her bed much earlier than normal and attempted to locate the source of this putrid stench. After an exhaustive search, she discovered that the odor was strongest around the downstairs floor registers. This eventually led her to walk outside the house, where she noticed that someone had removed a crawl space vent. She looked through the opening and could see a couple dozen broken eggs scattered across the plastic sheeting covering the dirt. Mixed with the Georgia heat and humidity, these now rotten eggs exuded a smell that seemed to slap Penny across the face.

Who in the world would do such a thing? And why?

Then Penny thought about her conversation the previous week with Mr. Jim Sheffield, and she was pretty sure she had her answer. She called the police and reported the vandalism, asking for an officer to stop by. When the deputy came, he took pictures and plenty of notes. He even wrote down the comments Penny made about Jim wanting to buy her house. The deputy offered no promises, gave her his business card, and told her to call if she had any further information to help them in their investigation.

It was two weeks later when Penny awoke one night to a strange sound coming from her kitchen. She turned on every light and searched for the source, finally opening her pantry and discovering holes gnawed through several cereal boxes and packages of cookies. She looked on the floor and noticed droppings.

A rat. Or *rats*, with an s. *Ugh. I can't believe it*, she thought.

The next day, after calling an extermination company, Penny decided to stop by the Grant County Sheriff's office. She told her story to an unsuspecting deputy she happened to catch at his desk. He listened, nodded his head, and then said, "You know what, Ms. Rogers, I'm going to let you talk with Sheriff Peterman. I think he should hear this."

The deputy walked with Penny to Ralph's office, made the introductions, summarized Penny's story for the Sheriff, and then quickly exited. Ralph invited Penny to sit and said, "So, you're convinced that Jim Sheffield is to blame for your recent problems?"

"Absolutely."

"I've got to be honest with you, Ms. Rogers, in all my years of police work, this is the first time anyone has blamed their rat infestation on a criminal action."

"Don't forget about the eggs under my house."

"Probably just some teenagers playing a prank. Or some kind of dare. I wouldn't jump to any crazy conclusions. Look, Jim and I grew up together. I've spent a lot of time with Jim. Sure, he's been gone several years and maybe he's not exactly the same Jim I remember, but there's no way he'd do something like this. Just let us keep doing our investigation on the eggs. If anything else happens, please let me know."

Penny wasn't satisfied, but knew she would be wasting her breath trying to convince the Sheriff that Jim was attempting to run her out of her house. She thanked him for his time and left.

The Sheriff then called his old friend, Jim Sheffield. Ralph had, as expected, attended Mr. Sheffield's funeral, and there they had exchanged current cell phone numbers and promised to get together as soon as the dust had settled.

"Jim. It's Ralph Peterman."

"Well, hey Ralph. Good to hear from you. You ready to get together for that beer?"

"Look, let's do that soon, but I need to ask you something, and I need you to be honest with me. You doing stuff to harass the lady living in your old house?"

There was silence on the other end of the line.

"Listen to me, Jim. She just left my office. She told me about your offer to buy the home and how she thinks you've put eggs and rats in her crawl space. You need to back off, buddy."

"Ralph, since you're the Sheriff, I want you to hear me say that I absolutely deny any involvement in those issues that lady mentioned to you. But Ralph, since you're also my friend, can I ask you how much you enjoyed all the hours you spent at my house growing up?"

"No doubt, Jim. It was great."

"Ralph, your first kiss happened at my house, out by the pool with Shelly Bagwell!"

"I remember, Jim."

"And you drank your first beer at *my* house, out of *my* refrigerator, while seated in a lounge chair by *my* pool!"

"Jim, I was there. I remember all of that. But your claim on that house no longer exists."

"Aw, come on, Ralph. Wouldn't it be nice for me to be able to invite you over on a Friday night, sit by the pool, drink a few beers—of course, legally this time— and tell stories about the good old days? And Ralph, I don't know what that woman told you, but my offer to her was *waay* more than fair. I ain't trying to take nothing from her. I just think I belong in that house."

"Jim, be that as it may, I need you to back off. I really don't need this headache right now."

"Gotcha, Ralph. Look, let's figure out a time to grab that beer and real soon, okay?"

It was a week later when Penny came home, set her purse and coat on the counter, plopped onto her couch, and immediately noticed a gushing sound of running water. She quickly raced around, looking for a burst faucet or shower head. Finding nothing, she walked out her front door, around her home, and discovered that every outside spigot was wide open. Water was everywhere, her front and back yards were soaked, and she had no idea how long they'd been running and what her water bill would be the next month. She turned off every spigot, went inside, and made a crucial decision.

For the next month, she gave up her lazy mornings. Each day, she woke early, marched into her kitchen, and began baking. The first day, it was chocolate chip cookies. Before her shift at the All-American Cafe began, she stopped by the Sheriff's office.

"Is Sheriff Peterman in?" she asked a deputy.

"No, he's out on a call."

Penny then handed over a plate covered in foil, filled with cookies. "Can you leave these for him? I'm sure he'll be willing to share with the rest of you guys as well."

The next day, she made brownies and went by the office. This time the Sheriff was in. She was escorted into his office and set a plate of brownies on his desk.

"Ms. Rogers, thank you for this, and thank you for the cookies yesterday, but you need to know that I'm a married man."

Penny smiled. "Look, Sheriff, I'm sure you get women who come onto you all the time. However, I promise you I'm not one of them. I've had one love in my life, he died fifteen years ago, and I'll never love again."

"But you are definitely going to see my face around here often. I'm determined that you will become my friend. And that you will begin to see me as a person. Not just a citizen pestering you about my problems, but someone who doesn't deserve the kind of harassment she's getting from your friend Jim Sheffield. So, you can expect to see me a lot. And if it takes baked goods to earn favor with your deputies so that I can have access to you, then so be it."

She then turned and walked out of his office.

The next day, she brought muffins. Then, a breakfast casserole. Cinnamon rolls the following day. Pigs in a blanket. Biscuits. She quickly became a beloved individual around the Sheriff's station. More importantly, she became a friend in the eyes of Sheriff Ralph Peterman.

In the early hours of a Saturday morning, well before the sun rose over the city of Mapleton, Jim Sheffield quietly tiptoed through the bushes of Mrs. Johnson's backyard and found the opening leading to 130 Main Street. He knew every house within two blocks and the contour of every yard. He could navigate the trails and cut throughs with his eyes closed. On this dark, early morning, that knowledge served him well.

In his right hand, he carried a plastic five-gallon bucket, the contents secured with a lid. He walked slowly, toward the decking surrounding the pool of his old home, listening for any sounds or signs of watching eyes. Sensing none, he made his way to the side of the pool, knelt, and slowly removed the lid from his bucket.

He quickly backed away, and then with his foot kicked the bucket so that the opening hovered over the edge of the pool. Gradually, five water moccasins crawled out and dropped into the pool below.

Satisfied that his mission was complete, Jim turned and began to retrace his steps toward the path cutting through Mrs. Johnson's yard, and then down the street to his car waiting for him in the parking lot of the First Baptist Church.

But, before he could make his escape, a bright flashlight suddenly beamed in his eyes. He raised his arms, shielding the light from his face. "What? Who is that?" he nervously shouted.

"Jim, what in the world are you doing?" Jim let out a sigh of relief as he recognized the voice of his old friend. "Ralph, thank God it's just you. Look, I'm not doing anything. Just fooling around. About to head home."

"Jim, I saw everything. Especially those snakes now slithering over there in the pool. You know, Jim, if those snakes happen to be poisonous, this is more than just harassment. It might be attempted murder."

"Murder? Come on, Ralph. Don't be ridiculous. I'm just fooling around. How about you just let this thing go, you know, for old time's sake?"

"Or, how about you turn around and put your hands behind your back, Jim?"

"What? You've got to be kidding me, Ralph."

"Jim Sheffield, you're under arrest. You have the right to remain silent. Anything you say can and will be used against you in a court of law…"

QUESTIONS FOR DISCUSSION:

Ice-Breaker: Name a time when you really wanted something, were told "no," but you continued to pursue it until you got what you wanted.

1. What are some similarities between this story and the parable of Jesus? Differences?
2. Read Luke 11:5-8. What does this parable teach us about prayer?
3. When is it hardest to keep praying and not give up?
4. Read Luke 11:11-13. What do these verses say about our relationship with God?
5. Do you believe that your Heavenly Father wants to give you good things? If so, why, then, do some of our prayers go unanswered?
6. Read Luke 11:1-4. What do you think the disciples meant when they asked Jesus to teach them to pray? Is prayer something that can be taught?
7. What are the elements of the Lord's Prayer? When you pray, does it model the prayer of Jesus?
8. When is your prayer life the most vibrant? When do you struggle praying?
9. In these passages, Jesus offered the assurance that our Heavenly Father sees us and will reward us. What do you think it means to live for an "audience of one?" What are practical ways Christ-followers can do this?

CHAPTER 5
TAYLOR'S TREASURE
The Parable of the Hidden Treasure

"*The kingdom of heaven is like treasure hidden in a field. When a man found it, he hid it again, and then in his joy went and sold all he had and bought that field.*"

Matthew 13:44

A Few Comments...

This is my favorite parable told by Jesus, and for several reasons. First, it is the shortest. I'm incredibly impressed by how Jesus managed to pack so much truth into only two sentences, what is just one verse in our modern Bibles.

Second, this story connects with the thrill all of us can imagine in unexpectedly discovering an item or items of great value. After the recent passing of my father, I found among his effects a stock certificate dated from the 1800's. The document indicated ownership of 500 shares in a gold mining company. *Could this have been passed down from his great-grandparents? How much are these shares worth today? Am I about to become an incredibly wealthy individual?*

After numerous Google searches, those initial thoughts quickly slipped away. The certificate was nothing more than a novelty item. However, the thoughts of this unexpected find brought a lot of excitement.

Third, the parable contains a truth I often forget. I must continually remind myself that the gospel is the greatest treasure I will ever obtain, and it is worth any sacrifice. Far too many times, my heart becomes too enamored with fool's gold and costume jewelry; items that cannot bring me the deep joy found in the gospel.

Fourth, the man in this parable doesn't begrudgingly sell his possessions. Jesus made it clear: in his *joy* he went and sold all he had. This individual didn't see his sacrifices as sacrifices at all. The treasure he would gain was of far greater value than the possessions he sold.

I want to live like this man; joyfully doing whatever it takes to center my life around the great gospel treasure.

Perhaps another story from Mapleton will shed a little more light on this truth.

TAYLOR'S TREASURE

Carl Lundy grew up on the east side of Mapleton, in a section of town disparagingly known as "Burnt Hill." Burnt Hill was a rural area with two official trailer parks and a couple dozen other mobile homes thrown out into pastures or buried deep within tracts of land. Burnt Hill had more dirt than paved roads and, historically, produced enough moonshine to supply Grant and several other surrounding counties. However, around the turn of the millennium, moonshine gave way to crystal methamphetamine production and consumption. Meth addiction ravaged the area and most families who resided in Burnt Hill. The Grant County Sheriff's Department had unofficially decided to cease patrolling this part of town. Unless the residents caused trouble in other areas of the county, they were allowed to live as they wished.

Carl's father had been an alcoholic and drug addict. When Carl was eight, his father left their trailer to buy moonshine and cigarettes. He never came home, and no one ever saw him again. The rumor around Burnt Hill was that he attempted to steal moonshine from Wally Easom and ended up on the business end of Wally's twelve-gauge shotgun. Wally would never confirm or deny this story, and no one pressed him for more information. The Easom brothers were known to be a dirty, rough bunch who likely had numerous bodies buried on their land.

While Carl's father had brought only pain and heartache to the family, Carl's mother was an absolute saint. Although they continued to struggle financially, she was determined to keep Carl and his brother in school and on the straight and narrow. Carl graduated from high school and found a job working in the warehouse at Sanders Seating. The following year, he married his high school sweetheart, Heather, and two years later, they welcomed a daughter, Taylor.

At only 25 years old, Carl was promoted to "inventory specialist" at Sanders Seating. Although his title indicated a certain level of expertise, in reality he spent most of his time unpacking boxes of chair components and placing them on assembly lines. It certainly wasn't a glamorous job; however, Carl worked hard and provided a stable home for his wife and daughter. He had broken the family cycle of addiction and poverty. He'd managed to escape Burnt Hill.

His determination, hard work, and love for his family were all traits highlighted at his funeral when he suddenly and unexpectedly died just a few months after turning 30. As a child, Carl had been diagnosed with epilepsy. However, his seizures ceased during his teenage years. His mom frequently told friends that "Carl outgrew his epilepsy." When Carl experienced a sudden unexpected death in epilepsy (SUDEP) episode while at his home on a Saturday night, the doctors told Heather there was nothing they could have done to save his life. It was simply his time to go.

At 29 years old, Heather Lundy was a despondent and heartbroken widow who wanted nothing more than to crawl into her bed and sleep her days away. Except, she had little eight-year-old Taylor to consider. Heather knew she had to pull herself together and care for her daughter. Like Carl, she came from a broken, low-income family. Her mom and stepfather now lived somewhere in southwest Florida. She hadn't seen her birth father since she was in middle school. Heather had a few friends who offered to help babysit, clean her home, run errands, and anything else she needed during this difficult time. She appreciated their support but knew that she would have to forge her own path for herself and Taylor.

A few weeks after the funeral, Heather started a cleaning service. Although it was a one-woman operation, it allowed her to set her schedule and work during the school day. Heather managed to earn enough cleaning houses to continue paying the mortgage on the small home she and Carl purchased the year before his death. More importantly, she could be with Taylor in the evenings and on the weekends. Although certainly not ideal, it was the hand dealt to her. This was the best Heather could do.

Throughout her grammar and middle school years, Taylor Lundy never had trouble making friends. While her financial situation meant she didn't always have the most expensive clothes or the latest accessories, Taylor was kind and friendly to everyone. Her classmates were quick to invite her to birthday and swim parties. In middle school, she accompanied a couple of friends and their families on summer beach trips, Taylor's only opportunity for a vacation. Although her economic status was below that of many others in her grade, she was well-liked and typically included in social activities.

However, in high school, her situation began to change. In 9th grade, it became clear that Taylor was more than just a nice girl. She had become, as well, absolutely stunning. She possessed naturally blonde hair and light blue eyes—eyes with almost a hint of silver. Her perfectly smooth, bronze skin somehow managed to avoid the ubiquitous plague of teenage acne. She was athletically built yet perfectly feminine in form. Hers was the face one would expect to see adorning the pages of a trendy teenage fashion catalog.

As she walked the high school hallways, heads turned to admire her graceful, natural beauty. That is, at least by those in the male portion of the population. The girls in her school became increasingly jealous of the attention shown to Taylor. Although she dressed modestly and refrained from gratuitous flirting, she received constant requests for her phone number and a possible date. Only after numerous polite refusals and the oft-repeated phrase, "My mom won't allow me to date until I'm sixteen," did the continual entreats subside.

Still, her female friend pool diminished substantially,

mainly due to the efforts of Madison Albright. Madison lived in a large, historic home on Main Street; one that had been in her family for three generations. Her father, an attorney who grew up in Atlanta, married a Mapleton girl with deep roots in the community. Madison's maternal grandfather had owned and operated the only funeral home in Mapleton, one he had inherited from his father. They belonged to the country club and First Presbyterian Church. Madison's mom was a member of the Junior League. Her father was a Rotarian. If Mapleton had royalty, it was most certainly the Albrights.

Madison was accustomed to being the center of attention and the most popular girl in her grade. All the girls in her classes wanted invitations to Madison's house for a birthday party or spend the night get-together. The Albright's backyard held a swimming pool and a lawn with a large playhouse, slide, and swings that rivaled many public parks. Children could enjoy hours of entertainment at her home, and Madison learned early in life how to leverage her family's wealth for her own personal gain. Other girls knew that kowtowing to Madison's wishes would earn them an invite to the next fabulous event she had planned. If they somehow displeased Madison, they might find themselves standing outside of the preferred social circle.

Throughout their grammar school and middle school years, Madison and Taylor were only acquaintances. In their younger years, Taylor received invitations to Madison's birthday parties simply because every girl in her class received the same invite. However, Taylor had never been asked—nor did she desire—to attend a spend-the-night party at Madison's home. Madison's family lived both literally and figuratively on the other side of the tracks from Heather and her mom. Taylor never felt entirely comfortable going to Madison's house and being around her parents or their friends. Her kindness toward Madison typically earned her an invitation to birthday and end-of-school-year parties; however, Taylor was quite happy to remain outside of Madison's inner circle.

This amicable, almost neutral friendship status changed during their 9th-grade year. Taylor's transformation from a cute, sweet girl into a beautiful young lady was evident. While admired by the guys, this fact ignited tremendous jealousy in Madison Albright. Her princess status, she believed, was now threatened by this usurper to the throne. Madison was determined to use every resource at her disposal to demean, degrade, and belittle Taylor Lundy. However, she knew these efforts had to be subtle and calculated. She could not appear to be the jealous shrew. She would casually ice Taylor out of social events, drop rumors she supposedly heard from others, and carefully offer derogatory comments on Taylor's clothes and financial status. Madison had learned the art of cleverly and delicately dealing with one's adversaries. On numerous occasions, she'd observed these skills on full display in the way her mother dealt with social challenges. Every time, Mrs. Albright managed to get her way. Madison would as well.

The Albrights always came out on top.

During Taylor's 9th grade year in school, Heather Lundy decided to expand her cleaning schedule. Since Carl's passing, she'd restricted her services to school hours so she could be fully available for Taylor. However, as Taylor grew older, so did their family's expenses. Taylor's clothes, school activities, and social functions all added to their monthly budget requirements. Plus, food, utility, and insurance costs continued to rise. Heather had cut expenses everywhere possible, but it still wasn't enough. She needed to generate more income. Cleaning houses on Saturdays was her only option.

Through the referral of another client, Heather managed to secure a new house to clean: The Albright home on Main Street. Mrs. Albright was willing to pay well for Heather's services. There was just one firm stipulation: the home had to be completely cleaned in under two hours. She had social engagements and friends who would drop by, and she didn't want the noise of a vacuum or the hassle of avoiding a freshly mopped floor. Mrs. Albright demanded the cleaners to be in and out of her home quickly.

Heather looked at the house and knew cleaning it alone would typically take her four or five hours. She was a one-woman operation and had managed to avoid a lot of headaches by keeping it this way. Hiring an assistant would significantly cut into her earnings and create mounds of paperwork and tax issues.

However, she really wanted this new client and the promised wages. This one job would give her the monthly income she needed to make ends meet. Plus, if she managed to clean the house in only two hours, it would give her most of Saturday to spend with Taylor, run personal errands, or enjoy some downtime. This reality led Heather to explain the situation to her daughter and request Taylor's help to clean the Albright home on Saturday mornings. They could start early, finish well before lunch, and have the rest of the day to do whatever they wanted. As well, she agreed to split the money with Taylor, which was a generous offer considering that Heather was paying for all the cleaning supplies.

Taylor didn't mind hard work, but she really didn't want to clean Madison Albright's house. Madison had a subtle way of making derogatory comments and casting furtive, hateful glances at Taylor whenever they were in the same vicinity. She knew this would give Madison even more ammunition for her snide remarks.

Except, she really wanted to help her mom and understood that this was the best way to contribute to the family's needs. And the offer of splitting the money was a fantastic bonus. Taylor was finishing her 9th-grade year in school. Next year, she would get her driver's license. If she managed to save enough, perhaps she could purchase a cheap car. Or at least help with the insurance costs so that she could occasionally drive her mom's car. Although she could foresee Madison's inevitable sarcastic remarks and jeers, Taylor agreed to help her mom.

At the beginning of her 10th-grade year, students who participated in the Mapleton High School chorus received the news that they had been selected to perform at Disney World that December. Numerous high school choruses from across the country were invited to each sing three songs as part of Disney's Winter Holiday Festival of Lights. During the month, these groups would perform at certain venues throughout Magic Kingdom. The Mapleton High chorus planned to travel by charter bus to Disney, sing for approximately 15 minutes one afternoon, and then enjoy the different theme parks for four days. It was a rare opportunity, and there was a lot of buzz among the students about this upcoming trip.

However, even with the discounted ticket prices offered by Disney, the cost for students to participate was $900. Most families could afford to pay this fee. Heather Lundy, however, knew it would significantly stretch her budget to send Taylor on this trip. This opportunity would be only possible if Taylor used the money she earned from helping her mom clean the Albright's home on Saturdays.

Of course, this would mean Taylor would have to delay getting a car for herself, but if she wanted to go to Disney, then she would have to make that sacrifice.

And Taylor was most definitely willing to make that sacrifice. In part because she imagined it would be an exciting trip. Moreover, Taylor knew Jack Stephens planned on going. Jack was also in 10th grade, a chorus member, and was the first guy Taylor had ever really liked. Unlike most other guys in high school, he was kind, sincere, and displayed an unusual level of maturity for his age.

Taylor and Jack had been in classes together since the 3rd grade, but this year wasn't the same as the previous ones. They sat next to each other in chorus and at the same table during lunch every day. They talked, laughed, and looked at one another differently than in previous years. While she wasn't jumping into anything too quickly, she enjoyed spending time with him at school. And she was pretty sure he felt the same way.

Which is why she was willing to use half of the money she earned from cleaning to pay for the Disney Trip. She looked forward to sitting next to Jack on the bus and, perhaps, on a few roller coaster rides as well. Those four days would be well worth the financial sacrifice.

The jealousy and animosity Madison felt toward Taylor during their 9th-grade year increased exponentially the following August. For several months prior, Madison had her sights set on Jack Stephens. He had become, in her mind, the cutest boy in their grade. At the beginning of her high school career, she had determined to date an upperclassman. Perhaps even a senior, although she knew that relationship would end after graduation. She spent a significant amount of time during her freshman year scoping and evaluating but never settled on a target. That is, until the spring of that year. Surprisingly, the object of her desire wasn't an older boy but one who had been in her classes for years. She'd always considered Jack to be a nice guy, but during their 9th-grade year, he experienced a dramatic transformation. He grew five or six inches. He traded his glasses for contacts. His middle school acne suddenly disappeared. He filled out and seemed to finally fit into his body.

The more she thought about it, the more sense it made to date someone who would be around for her entire high school career. She knew the other girls in their grade had taken notice of Jack and that he was becoming an A-lister at their school. Together, they would be the "it couple" at Mapleton High School.

However, Jack was completely unresponsive to her flirtations, invites, and suggestions. He was always kind. And friendly. But either clueless or not interested. Madison had a lot of trouble believing that the latter could be the case. She considered herself very attractive and engaging, and her family was wealthy. Madison had lots of friends and had always enjoyed a high-level of popularity among her peers. In her mind, she could date most any upperclassman, so surely a boy in her own grade would be flattered to know that she was interested in him, right?

Yet, Jack had wholly disregarded Madison's advances. Quite shockingly, he seemed to be spending a lot of time with Taylor Lundy, which made no sense at all to Madison. Sure, Taylor was attractive in a poor, simple kind of way, but she wore cheap clothes and inexpensive accessories. And she lived on the other side of the railroad tracks in a part of town known as the Old Mill Village. Madison's bedroom was nearly as big as Taylor's entire home. Undoubtedly, Jack—whose family belonged to the country club and lived on her side of town—wasn't interested in this girl, was he?

Madison was going to find out. And she would win this battle. She knew she would.

Albrights always came out on top.

It was the last Saturday in September when Taylor and her mom pulled into the driveway of the Albright home just before 9:00 a.m. "Look," Heather said, "I know this isn't exactly the ideal job, cleaning the home of one of your classmates. But it's good money and I promise you that hard work never hurt anyone."

"I know, Mom. It's just Madison is so… well, she's just Madison. I really hope she's not home."

"Mrs. Albright said that Madison had cheer practice this morning and would not be here. Mrs. Albright is going to let us in and then run some errands. We are supposed to be done by 11:00 a.m. We can do it if we work quickly. I need to keep this account."

Heather had already outlined a game plan for attacking the job. If Taylor would vacuum, sweep, and mop, her mom would handle the rest of the cleaning. Her first task was to vacuum the upstairs portion of the house. Four bedrooms and an upstairs den had floors with the most expensive-looking carpet Taylor had ever seen. The plush, thick, cream-colored wool must have cost a fortune. She removed her shoes before entering the house—a requirement of Mrs. Albright—and when Taylor walked across the carpeted floors in her socks, it felt like a down comforter under her feet. She never imagined she would enjoy vacuuming until this moment.

She started in the master bedroom, moved to the two guest rooms, and then the upstairs den. The last room she vacuumed was Madison's, and she had to spend 20 minutes moving clothes and other items to the bed and closet before she could see the floors hiding under all the clutter.

When she picked up a pair of Golden Goose sneakers and placed them in the walk-in closet, she happened to notice a box on the floor. The flaps were pulled back, and she could see it was full of record albums. She turned to continue cleaning, but suddenly stopped. The album sitting on top of the stack caught her eye. She leaned down and noticed that it was The Beatles—their 1966 "Yesterday and Today" compilation.

Taylor was immediately transported back to a time when she was just a little girl, before her father passed away, listening to albums on her father's record player. Carl Lundy loved The Beatles. And Sam Cooke, Elton John, Elvis, and Prince. He talked about the distinct sound of a record not heard on tapes, CD's, or MP3's. He would open the album covers, read about the artists, and admire the quality of the vinyl record.

As well, he discussed the value of rare albums and the hopes that one day he might stumble upon one of these at an estate sale or hidden in the back of an old antique store. He'd researched the true collectibles and knew the approximate value of each. Because Heather had grown tired of hearing his long-winded descriptions of these albums, Carl decided to share his thoughts with little Taylor. While she lacked a complete understanding of the details, she loved watching her father's excitement and the fact that he wanted to talk with her about this important subject. So, she sat quietly, and her young mind soaked up her father's words.

This is how Taylor immediately knew the value of this album staring her in the face. She leaned down and carefully pulled up one side of this top album to see what was underneath. It was Prince's "Black Album," one her father had discussed numerous times. Prince was unhappy with this recording, called it "too dark" and demanded all the copies be destroyed. A few survived, however, and Taylor found herself in the presence of a hidden gem.

She moved her thumb underneath this album and gently lifted it to one side. The next one in the stack was The Rolling Stones, "Street Fighting Man," a single released in 1968. Yet another story she remembered hearing from her father. The cover featured harsh police intervention during a protest. Most radio stations refused to play the song in the aftermath of the riots at the Democratic National Convention that same year. Most of the albums were destroyed, but her father told her a few survived, and any one of those in decent shape would likely sell for thousands.

Taylor's heart raced as she mentally calculated the value of what she had just seen, knowing there were many more albums below. She started thumbing through a few more when she suddenly heard an insistent, harsh voice ask, "What EXACTLY do you think you're doing?"

Taylor turned and saw Madison standing in the doorway to her bedroom. She was wearing shorts and a tank top, her hands on her hips, and a scowl on her face. Taylor froze as Madison practically screamed, "Are you going through my stuff?!?"

"No, no. I mean, kinda. Really, I was just putting your shoes in your closet so I could vacuum, and I noticed this open box. I was curious, so I leaned down to see what was in it. I'm so sorry. I didn't mean to snoop."

"Well, you were," Madison said, this time with a little less anger, but with an exasperated tone. "I mean, you're SUPPOSED to be cleaning, not looking through my closet."

"I know, I know, and I'm so sorry. I just saw the albums and thought…"

"You mean you were looking at those old, dusty records my grandfather left for me in his will? I have no idea why I haven't thrown those out yet. My cousins all got these hefty trust accounts when he died, but for some reason I got an old box full of outdated music. I keep meaning to do something with that junk. I need to make more room in my closet anyway."

"Ummm, well, if you don't want them, maybe I could buy the box from you."

"Really? You want to buy ALL the albums? You don't even know what is in there. You didn't flip through the whole box, did you?"

"No, but I just like vinyl albums. I still have my dad's old record player and his music collection. I like to play it sometimes and remember when we would listen to an album, and he would share the stories behind the bands and the songs."

Madison smiled, thinking about this opportunity that had suddenly presented itself. When Mrs. Albright told her that Taylor would be helping clean the house, she had sternly lectured her daughter about being polite and not treating a classmate like a servant. Madison agreed but insisted that she know the reason why Taylor Lundy would be cleaning their home. Mrs. Albright informed her that Heather could not afford to pay for Madison to go on the chorus trip to Disney, but Taylor really wanted to go. And this Saturday morning job would provide her with enough money to pay for the trip.

Madison also knew that Taylor wanted to go to Disney so that she could spend time with Jack Stephens. And that Jack likely wanted Taylor to go. However, if Madison could somehow keep Taylor off the chorus trip, surely she could use her feminine prowess to turn Jack's attention to her. She was, after all, Madison Albright.

And Albrights always came out on top.

"Tell you what," Madison said. "I'll sell the albums to you."

"Okay. How much?"

"$1,500."

"What? Just a few moments ago, you said you wanted to throw out the box!"

"I know," Madison said as she feigned a doleful expression. "But I loved my grandfather so much, and I can't just give these albums away. They meant a great deal to him. I feel like I owe it to his memory to place a high value on his collection. $1,500 seems like a lot for a box of old albums, but it represents his musical journey." Madison's voice trailed away as if this were a sentimental moment for her.

Taylor thought about her options. The check for the chorus trip was due that Monday. Her mom had agreed to front the money but was clear that Taylor had to pay her back from this cleaning job, and quickly, so that her mom would have enough to pay their property tax and insurance bills, both due at the end of October. But even if she managed to convince her mom to give her the cash instead of paying for the trip, she was still $600 short. She had to figure something out, and quickly.

"Madison, I'll be back this afternoon with your money."

"You want to do WHAT?!?" Heather practically screamed as they rode away from the Albright home. "I don't understand at all. The chorus trip is all you've talked about since the first day of school."

"I know, Mom. But you need to trust me on this. I need the $900, and if I could borrow $600 more, I *promise* I'll pay you back."

"I don't have $600 more. This money from the cleaning today is the only reason I can write a check for $900 on Monday. After that check clears, I'm down to $45 in my account."

"Ugh. I don't know what to do."

"How about you don't spend a ridiculous amount of money on a box of old records. I know you miss your father and that he was nuts about vinyls, but we are not in a financial place to purchase nonessentials."

"Mom," Taylor quickly replied. "Can you run to the bank, cash the check from Mrs. Albright and then give me what you were going to pay for the chorus trip?

Then, I need you to take me home and later run some errands with me."

"Taylor, you're acting crazy. This isn't like you."

"I know it isn't, Mom. Which is why I need you to trust me right now."

They quickly made it to the bank before it closed at noon. After racing home, Taylor went through her room and boxed nearly every item of clothing she owned. She then put her jewelry in another box. She grabbed her make-up case, a couple of lamps, and three dolls she'd owned for years. Other items went into boxes and into the car.

Taylor and her mom drove to Jane's Closet, a thrift store in Mapleton that purchased used clothes. The owner looked through the boxes of jackets, jeans, and shoes. At one point, the owner pulled out Taylor's fake Prada jacket, a gift from her mom that looked to be genuine. Taylor believed it to be authentic and proudly wore it to school on the first day of 9th grade. At lunch, Madison Albright pointed out that if you looked closely, the "P" was actually a "B."

"Brada," Madison laughed, making sure the other girls at the table could hear her side of the conversation. "Sounds more like an undergarment than jacket!"

Taylor never wore it again. The jacket hung in the back of her closet for over a year. Now, it was in the hands of Jane, being evaluated along with the other items.

"Tell you what," she said, "I'll give you $100 for all of it."

"That's it?" Taylor replied. "Only $100?"

"Take it or leave it. I've got other customers I need to assist."

Taylor took it. She needed $500 more.

They raced to the other side of town, to Westside Pawn and Jewelry. Taylor and her mom carried in the boxes containing the items Taylor had gathered from her room. The man behind the counter looked like a real shyster, the kind of guy who would sell his own mother for the right price. He sifted through the items, including the jewelry, and offered a paltry $200 for everything. "What?" Taylor said, "You'll end up selling all of this stuff for triple that amount!"

"Of course I will. That's how I make a living. Do you want the money or not?"

"Is there any way you can go to $500?"

"Sure. If the diamond on that necklace you're wearing is real, I will give you another $300. It's small, but I'll be able to get a nice price for it."

"Yes, it's real. My dad gave this to me for my birthday when I turned eight. I can't part with this."

"Then I can't part with the extra $300." The way he said that sentence, it was like he was enjoying the moment.

Taylor knew she was out of options. She removed the necklace and handed it over. The owner quickly inspected it, verified its authenticity, and then reached into the cash register and handed five crisp $100 bills over to Taylor. "Nice doing business with you," he said.

Taylor and her mom turned and quickly left the store.

"I've never seen anything like this," said Nick Putnall, owner of Record Warehouse in the Buckhead area of Atlanta. "Where did you get these?"

"I purchased the entire box from a girl who really didn't want them."

"I hope you got a receipt clearly showing you'd paid for the items. I would hate for her to make a claim on them now."

Taylor pulled it out. She was careful to document the transaction with Madison.

"You mean you only paid $1,500 for this entire box?!?"

"That was what she asked."

"Girl, you got the deal of a lifetime. You never know what these will go for at an auction, but I guarantee this box is worth over $500,000. Likely more. This is an unbelievable collection."

"I know," Taylor said. "My father taught me a lot about records."

"I'm happy to help you sell these, if that's what you want. I've done this plenty of times before for other customers, but never with albums of this caliber. Let me get a contract and we can talk specifics."

Neither Taylor nor Heather ever cleaned the Albright home again.

Taylor was able to purchase her necklace back from Westside Pawn and Jewelry for "the discounted rate" of only $600.

Although her payment was a few days late, Taylor got a check to her teacher for the Christmas chorus trip to Disney.

Taylor and Jack became the "it couple" at Mapleton High School.

Taylor purchased a real Prada jacket. She never wore a fake knock-off again.

And, for the first time ever, the Lundy's came out on top.

QUESTIONS FOR DISCUSSION:

Ice-Breaker: Can you think of a time you had to make a major sacrifice to get something you really wanted? Describe that experience.

1. What are some similarities between this story and the parable of Jesus? Differences?
2. Notice the word "joy" in the verse. Why did the man experience joy as he sold all his possessions?
3. Read Matthew 13:45-46. What are some similarities between this parable and the prior one told by Jesus? What are some differences?
4. The merchant in the second parable was likely a buyer who had become an expert on pearls. Why is this detail significant?
5. These two parables are the shortest Jesus told, yet they have a powerful point. What did Jesus want his listeners to understand by telling these parables?
6. Read Matthew 10:37-39. What do these verses say about following Jesus?
7. Read Matthew 16:24. What does this verse say about following Jesus?
8. What are sacrifices we must make to follow Christ? What sacrifices are the hardest for you? Have you ever thought the sacrifices might not be worth it?
9. Read Luke 18:18-23. What does this story teach us about those who aren't willing to make sacrifices to follow Christ?

10. Do you value Christ as much as the individuals in the story valued the buried treasure and the perfect pearl?

CHAPTER 6
STEVE'S SCHEME
The Parable of the Shrewd Manager

J*esus told his disciples:* "There was a rich man whose manager was accused of wasting his possessions. So he called him in and asked him, 'What is this I hear about you? Give an account of your management, because you cannot be manager any longer.'

"The manager said to himself, 'What shall I do now? My master is taking away my job. I'm not strong enough to dig, and I'm ashamed to beg—I know what I'll do so that, when I lose my job here, people will welcome me into their houses.'

"So he called in each one of his master's debtors. He asked the first, 'How much do you owe my master?'

"'Nine hundred gallons of olive oil,' he replied.

"The manager told him, 'Take your bill, sit down quickly, and make it four hundred and fifty.'

"Then he asked the second, 'And how much do you owe?'

"'A thousand bushels of wheat,' he replied.

"He told him, 'Take your bill and make it eight hundred.'

"The master commended the dishonest manager because he had acted shrewdly. For the people of this world are more shrewd in dealing with their own kind than are the people of the light. I tell you, use worldly wealth to gain friends for yourselves, so that when it is gone, you will be welcomed into eternal dwellings.

NOT SO FAR, FAR AWAY

Luke 16:1-9

A Few Comments...

This is a hard parable and one that can easily confuse the reader. There is a manager who is accused of being wasteful by his wealthy employer. The employee does not deny this accusation. Evidently, he had not been a good steward with the master's resources. He is then dismissed from his position.

On the heels of his termination, this manager calls upon those who owe his now-former employer money. He quickly and substantially reduces their debts to curry favor with these individuals. *Perhaps*, he thought, *they will reward my kindness with the offer of employment.*

The employer sees these actions of his manager, and instead of calling the police or taking him before a judge, he praises the man for his shrewdness.

What?!?

Stealing, cheating, and looking out for one's own self-interests seem to be praised by Jesus in this parable. It's not at all what we expect.

However, when you put this parable into its proper context, it makes sense. Almost immediately following this parable is the story of the rich man and Lazarus. This rich man has many fine things in life, but none can save him from the awful torture he experiences after death. The wealthy individual failed to act "shrewdly" with his worldly possessions.

This is the main point of Jesus. Where the shrewd manager was able to use money to secure a future for himself, we can use money to "lay up treasures in heaven" (Matthew 6:20). When you plan for your financial future, do so for your eternal future as well.

When you read this parable, don't get caught up in the details of the manager's actions. Rather, focus on the central truth Jesus taught. We all know that the end of our lives will come. If we are half as shrewd as this manager, we will use our financial resources to gain future rewards.

Perhaps an event in Mapleton's history will help us see this idea in a new light.

STEVE'S SCHEME

Throughout Mapleton—in every diner and hair salon, in churches, at the country club, in teachers' lounges at the schools—rumors swirled regarding what would become of Sanders Seating after the death of Mr. Barry Sanders. Other than the county government, Sanders Seating was the largest employer in Mapleton. Barry's father, Barry Sr., started the business in the early 1960s. Over the decades, Sanders Seating had become the number one supplier of chairs for school systems throughout the southeast. When Barry Sr., a.k.a. "Big Barry," unexpectedly passed in 1994, his son became the President and CEO of Sanders Seating. Big Barry's widow happily received a check from the company each month but had zero interest in the day-to-day affairs of running the business. The transition was nearly seamless since Barry Jr. had already spent two years working at Sanders Seating. Most employees saw very few changes in their job duties or company processes.

However, when Little Barry unexpectedly died in 2017, there was no clear succession plan for the management of Sanders Seating. Barry's oldest child, Trey, was only 11 years old. His widow, Ashley, inherited the company, but she hadn't worked in over a dozen years. Moreover, she had zero interest in running the business. Or, for that matter, staying in Mapleton. She planned on moving to her hometown of Marietta, Georgia, as quickly as possible. The day after the funeral, her attorney scheduled a meeting with a commercial broker about selling Sanders Seating. Ashley Sanders was already a billionaire, and the sale of this business would add millions to her net worth.

During the transition, the company's leadership fell to Steve Williamson, a lifelong resident of Mapleton and a twenty-five-year veteran of Sanders Seating. When Barry Jr. took over the business at only 24 years of age, he immediately promoted Steve from shift manager to Chief Operating Officer. Barry had watched his father figuratively and literally kill himself by micromanaging the company's operations. Nothing happened at Sanders Searing without Big Barry's approval. If the custodian wanted to change cleaning supplies, he would ask Mr. Sanders before doing so. Every shift operator filled out a daily log highlighting issues with employees, machinery, or supplies. Every morning, Barry reviewed these documents and decided on any necessary changes or adjustments.

Barry Jr.'s leadership style differed greatly from his father's. While he worked just as hard and as many hours, he focused his energy on expanding the business and big-picture issues. He didn't care what kind of cleaning supplies the custodian used. He didn't need to know if a machine operator missed a shift because of a sick child. He would not concern himself with low inventory. To grow the business, he knew he had to devote his time and energy to customers, marketing, and learning more about the latest technology. Reading daily logs would not be part of his morning routine.

Which is precisely why Barry promoted Steve Williamson to the newly created position of COO. Steve would be the one to read reports, manage vacation days, order supplies, and handle the hundreds of other decisions required for the business to run successfully. Barry and Steve worked together for two years before Big Barry passed away. During that time, Barry had observed Steve's character and competency. He not only believed Steve could get the job done, but Barry knew him to always be honest and fair. Steve was paid well to manage the day-to-day affairs of Sanders Seating.

Barry and Steve met for lunch every Monday afternoon in Barry's office. Steve handed his boss a report with an overview of the previous week's activities, including payments received, outstanding invoices, shipments fulfilled, and any issues with personnel, property, or machinery. Barry would read the document, ask a few questions, and occasionally give some direction or input into a problem. Their meetings rarely lasted more than an hour. After this time, Barry could return to researching new marketing ideas, reading about the latest technology in manufacturing, or placing phone calls to school superintendents around the country. They were a great team and, together, had managed to grow Sanders Seating into a multimillion-dollar business.

Then, Barry Sanders passed away. While the operations continued under Steve's leadership, the tension in the company and throughout Mapleton was palpable. What would happen to this economic backbone of the town? If Sanders Seating closed or moved, would tax revenues decline so significantly that the school system would be forced to cut teachers' salaries? Or slice the budgets for sporting and other extracurricular activities? What about police, fire, and medical services? Residents worried that Mapleton would become a ghost town if Sanders Seating left.

Fortunately, all those fears were allayed when it was announced that Ashley Sanders had agreed to sell the business to Red Mountain Investments, a private equity group headquartered in Birmingham, Alabama. RMI owned more than a dozen manufacturing companies throughout the southeast. They typically acquired a business, worked to improve efficiency, and, ultimately, increase profits. Then, usually three to seven years later, they would sell the company at a significantly higher price than what they'd paid.

In the case of Sanders Seating, Ashley was ready to sell and, honestly, didn't need the money, anyway. RMI made her a lower-than-market offer, and she quickly accepted. She was anxious to wash her hands of Sanders Seating and Mapleton, which gave RMI an incredible opportunity. As their CEO stated to the board, they had already made their money going into the deal. Improving the company's bottom line and making it worth more would simply be icing on the cake.

It was a win-win for everyone involved.

STEVE'S SCHEME

Between the time of Barry's death and the sale of Sanders Seating, Steve Williamson—at the request of Ashley Sanders—became the acting CEO of the company. The change minimally affected his job duties. For more than two decades, Steve had run the day-to-day operations of Sanders Seating. All the employees breathed a sigh of relief, knowing that Steve would remain in charge, at least for a little while. The company could easily continue production and shipping their products under Steve's leadership. In this interim period, Steve was free to run Sanders Seating just as he and Barry had for years.

However, this changed almost immediately after the sale of the company to RMI. Eric Kinsey walked into Steve's office and introduced himself as the "Vice President for Corporate Growth." Eric could not have been more than 30 years old. He quickly informed Steve that he had been with the company for two years after working in New York City for almost five years managing a hedge fund. Before that, he'd completed his MBA at Harvard after receiving his undergraduate degree in finance from George Washington. He freely admitted to knowing nothing about manufacturing plastic chairs but claimed to know a lot about how to make profits. RMI, he stated, sent him to this backwoods town to make Sanders Seating more efficient and profitable. His job was to take this dull little penny and make it as shiny as possible. Once he'd accomplished this, the company would be resold, and he and RMI would move on to another project.

He never once asked Steve a personal question. He asked very few professional questions. Eric Kinsey wanted it known that *he* was now in charge.

Steve listened to Eric—who insisted that Steve and all other employees call him "Mr. Kinsey"—bloviate for over an hour about who he was and what he would do at Sanders Seating. Then he left Steve's office to settle into his new office, the one with the nameplate "Barry Sanders" still attached to the door.

"I really, really hate this guy," Steve declared to his wife that evening while they dined on meatloaf and mashed potatoes. "I mean *hate*. I don't know that I've ever been in the presence of someone who has made my skin crawl so much. He is an arrogant imbecile. He only wanted to talk about his fancy degrees and how much money he had made for RMI. He didn't ask my opinion on anything. I've been running this company with Barry for the last twenty years, not that he cares about that fact or anything else I might have to say. I think I'm going to quit."

"And do what?" she asked.

"I don't know. Something else. Anything else. Some job where I don't have to listen to this kid, barely past puberty, telling me how to run the company."

"Honey, this is Mapleton, Georgia. There aren't

many jobs around here paying what you're making right now. Didn't you tell me that they ultimately want to resell the company anyway? Can't you hang on until that happens?"

"That could be years," Steve practically shouted, pieces of mashed potatoes spewing from his mouth.

"Maybe. Or maybe not. Or maybe RMI replaces this Mr. Kinsey…"

"Eric," Steve interrupted.

"What?"

"I might have to call him 'Mr. Kinsey' at the office, but at home that snot-nosed little punk will be called, 'Eric.'"

"Okay, okay. So, what if RMI replaces *Eric*. Or what if little Eric decides to leave for another career opportunity? And then you've quit this job that really pays well."

"Yeah, I guess you're right."

"And, if you hate Eric this much, how do you think the other employees are going to feel about him? Are you going to jump ship and leave those other guys to deal with Eric? Sure, with your background and experience, you could probably find another job. But a lot of those guys are stuck. They will have no choice but to follow Eric's commands, without you there to stand up for them."

"Alright. You've said enough. I'll at least try and stick it out for a little while longer."

"Steve, I've been studying the personnel files, and we've got a big problem," Eric said, never looking directly at Steve. Instead, he pointed and glared at a sheet of paper resting on the desk in front of him.

"I'm listening. What's the issue?" Steve and his new boss were now into the third hour of their Monday morning meeting. Steve never missed Barry more than at this moment. He longed for the brevity of his old employer. He missed having lunch in this office. Eric demanded they meet at 7:00 a.m., and didn't offer so much as a cup of coffee. *This is miserable,* Steve thought to himself. *I don't know how much longer I can put up with this guy.*

"You see," Eric said as if he were an elementary school teacher explaining long division to a child, "Only 20% of the workforce at Sanders Seating is under 40. And over a quarter of the employees are over 60. And nearly half are between 50 and 60 years old."

"And this is a problem because…?"

"Because Steve!" Eric practically shouted. "You have to pay older workers substantially more than younger workers! And in the case of Sanders Seating, the long tenure of our employees is killing us. Most of these over-fifty guys have spent their entire careers with this company. They have received COLA raises and merit raises that have compounded over the years, and therefore are pulling in really good salaries. Heck," Eric said as he pointed to a name on the sheet of paper. "This Mr. Randy Hillbrook fellow is getting paid six figures to be the plant superintendent. We could hire a younger guy for two-thirds the cost of what we are paying him."

"I've known Randy for a long time, and he is an outstanding employee. Plus, he is super loyal to the company."

"Be that as it may, this seems to be the situation across the board. From Randy down to the night custodians, these salaries are *waaay* higher than what we should be paying employees here in a place like Mapleton, Georgia. I did a little research, and the employees of Sanders Seating are making, on average, 20% more than the median salary in Grant County."

"Look, Mr. Kinsey, I don't doubt your statistics. I've personally not done a deep dive into the numbers, but I'm sure you're correct. However, while we spend a little more on our personnel, I think this saves us money in other areas. For one, we rarely spend funds on hiring and training new employees. When we do, we normally let them shadow one of our veterans, and production output continues to remain strong. If I have to squander hours reviewing resumes, doing background checks, and setting up training seminars, it will take away from our bottom line."

"As well, Barry did a great job building a culture of trust and camaraderie here. Do you know that in the last 20 years, we've only had two workers' comp claims? If one of these guys twists his ankle on the job, he doesn't bother with workers' comp. He just goes to his doctor, lets his insurance handle it, and is normally back to work the next day. The men and women who work here are paid well; they know it, but they are also fiercely loyal to the company."

"Not to mention that these employees do excellent work. The reason Sanders Seating sells more plastic chairs than anyone else in the southeast isn't just because Barry was a great salesman. We have a superior product here, due in large part to the fact that our employees actually care about what we are making. They aren't going to let a chair slip through the assembly line that will end up falling apart later when it's sitting in a school somewhere."

"Mr. Kinsey, I don't doubt at all your business knowledge. However, respectfully, the man who occupied this office for years knew how to make a lot of money, and he did so with the employees you see out there right now. My grandfather always said, 'If it ain't broke, don't fix it.' Again, respectfully, I think you're trying to fix something that ain't broke."

Eric Kinsey sat motionless, staring hard at Steve with a look of absolute disgust on his face. "Steve, I guess you know a thing or two about how to make plastic chairs, but you know nothing about taking a company and dressing it up to sell in the commercial marketplace. If you want to remain an employee of Red Mountain, I suggest you stay in your lane. I don't need your advice on how to make this company more profitable."

"As well, Steve, I am going to give you a list of individuals who need to be managed out of the company. We'll give them a small severance package, but we can't keep them on at such high salaries. I've already put out ads for open positions—ones that technically won't be open until we let these other employees go. We can work on a way to give them a bonus if they will train their replacements. Sure, they will gripe and complain. But in my experience, they will do what we ask because they need that money."

"Mr. Kinsey, that is ruthless. I know you said you didn't want my opinion, but I think this is a huge mistake."

"Steve, you're exactly right. I don't want your opinion. I'll get the list to you this afternoon. We are done here. Thank you for your time."

Steve sat across the table from Dan Carter at the All-American Cafe. Steve and Dan weren't close, but they had developed a professional relationship over the last decade. Dan served as the school superintendent for the Grant County School District and, on numerous occasions, had pleaded with Barry Sanders to give the county a financial break on the purchase of chairs for the schools. Barry refused, saying, "Even if my own mama wants to buy ten plastic chairs, she will pay the same price as everyone else. I do not want to slide down the slippery slope of giving deals to certain individuals, companies, or government entities. Plus," he added, "Both I and my company contribute greatly to the county through taxes."

Dan thought about buying chairs from one of Barry's competitors; however, the amount he saved on shipping by purchasing local was substantial. He was, though, always a little bitter that Barry wouldn't cut him a deal.

"Look," Dan said to Steve as their food arrived. "I'm not asking for some great deal. But we are trying to build a new field house for the football field over in Rockdale, and all my teachers want raises, and I still need to purchase chairs for five of the elementary schools in the county. And the county commissioners refuse to raise taxes, which I understand. They must answer to their neighbors and friends and fellow church members about an increase in property taxes. I'm just trying to figure out how to give everyone what they are asking for with the limited funds available to me."

"Barry wouldn't budge on the price, but Barry's not around anymore. Is there anything you can do for me?"

"Dan, what is the total cost for the chairs you need to order?"

Dan pulled a pen out of his pocket, wrote a number on the napkin beside his plate, and slid it over to Steve.

"Whew, that's a lot of chairs you're buying."

"Have to. The ones we are replacing were purchased when Barry was still in high school. But any break would help me tremendously on raises and making that field house more than just a cinderblock building."

"Got it. Do this. Call me on Monday to put in the order. I'll give you the chairs at cost. That will cut your bill in half."

"What? Really? Come on, Steve. You're pulling my leg. Can you do that?"

"I'll have to get Mr. Kinsey to sign off on it, but he won't even notice. He's hyper- focused right now on reducing costs. He signs the order sheets and barely looks at them."

"Wow, Steve. Thanks so much. You know, I've always admired the way you supported Barry and the success the two of you had together. I sure wish I could steal you away. We need a Human Resources Officer at the Central Office. It pays well and you would answer directly to me. I know you've been with Sanders for a long time and probably have zero interest in this position, but I sure could use a guy like you."

"Dan, I might just take you up on that offer. Let me see what happens in the next month or so. We'll be in touch."

It was early on a Monday morning when Eric Kinsey sat in a large boardroom on the twentieth floor of a building in downtown Birmingham, one owned by Red Mountain Investments, Inc. Exactly twelve men and women—all executives with various titles and responsibilities over the different divisions of the company—were seated around a massive, heavy, mahogany table in a room covered with woodwork stained a deep, rich brown. It was the quarterly meeting of the top brass. Although Eric was the least tenured employee in the room, he spoke with nearly unbridled arrogance and always managed to position himself close to Thomas Benefield, the President and CEO of the company.

It was during a break when Eric began joking about his 'prison sentence' in Mapleton, a town he described as "Podunk, backward, and full of rednecks." Although these words were spoken to Harrison Caldwell, the Chief Financial Officer, they were overheard by Mr. Benefield, seated only a few feet away.

Several minutes later, Eric felt a tap on his shoulder. He turned and saw Thomas Benefield standing behind him. "Mr. Kinsey, may I have a word outside?"

Once in the hallway, Mr. Benefield said, "Eric, how long have you been with Red Mountain now? Two years?"

"Yes, sir. That's correct."

"And, when you were interviewing with our company, I'm sure you did some research on me. Did you know I went to Northwestern for my undergrad and received my MBA from Columbia?"

"Absolutely. I remember that well. Two great schools."

"You're right. Two great schools. And I loved my time in Chicago and in New York. However, in your investigation, did you happen to find out where I grew up?"

"Yes, I remember reading that you call Georgia your home. Atlanta, right?"

"Yes, on Georgia, but wrong on Atlanta. I grew up in Cedartown, which is only about a two-hour drive from here. It's a small town in northwest Georgia, one you would probably call "Podunk, backward, and full of rednecks." However, that is not how I would describe it. It's a place where people are kind, neighborly, and willing to help someone in need. It's where I learned both the value of hard work and the danger of putting money ahead of people."

"And one of the most valuable lessons I learned was understanding how to keep my opinion to myself, especially if I didn't know the background of others in the room."

"Now, Mr. Kinsey, here is where you come in. I've read your proposal on Sanders Seating, and it's perhaps the dumbest idea I've seen in all my years at Red Mountain. This is a highly profitable manufacturer, and yet you want to completely gut the workforce that has built it into what it is today."

"We bought Sanders Seating because we got it well below market value. We purchased it for what it is, not some potential you think might be there if we reduce payroll costs."

"However, I do see the benefit, at times, of cutting employees. Like right now."

"You're fired, Mr. Kinsey."

QUESTIONS FOR DISCUSSION:

Ice-Breaker: Have you ever been the victim of a con or ripped-off in some way? Describe that experience.

1. What are some similarities between this story and the parable of Jesus? Differences?
2. What are ways in which we can be shrewd in our Christian walk?
3. Read Luke 16:19-31. Jesus told this parable almost immediately after the parable of the shrewd manager. Do you think they are related? Why or why not?
4. In the parable of the rich man and Lazarus, was the rich man being shrewd in how he dealt with his wealth? Did he think long-term in the way he approached his money?
5. Read Luke 6:22-23. What did Jesus say in these verses about suffering and heaven? How does this relate to the parable of the shrewd manager?
6. Read Luke 6:35. What did Jesus say in this verse about future rewards for those who do good to their enemies? Does this change how you approach those who mistreat you?
7. Read Luke 14:12-14. What did Jesus say about our actions now and the reward we will receive later?
8. What are some practical ways you can remind yourself to be shrewd about your faith journey?

CHAPTER 7
CADEN'S CURVE
The Parable of the Wise and Foolish Builders

"Therefore everyone who hears these words of mine and puts them into practice is like a wise man who built his house on the rock. The rain came down, the streams rose, and the winds blew and beat against that house; yet it did not fall, because it had its foundation on the rock. But everyone who hears these words of mine and does not put them into practice is like a foolish man who built his house on sand. The rain came down, the streams rose, and the winds blew and beat against that house, and it fell with a great crash."

Matthew 7:24-27

A Few Comments...

This is, arguably, the most direct, easy-to-understand parable of Jesus. His disciples never had to ask, "Can you tell us the meaning of this parable?" His point was crystal clear.

However, it may be the most challenging one to apply to our lives. Even seasoned Christians struggle with the temptation to build our lives on the wrong foundation.

Often, it's a career. *If I succeed in my job, then I'll be secure.*

Or it's financial gain. *With enough money in the bank or my 401(k), I can weather any storm.*

Perhaps it's a relationship. *If I can find the right person, I can face whatever comes my way. As long as this individual sticks beside me, I'll be just fine.*

Maybe it's the approval of others, staying physically fit, or serving in a cause that makes a difference in our world. We believe we will find fulfillment in these pursuits. We place our hopes in their fruits.

Yet, the application of this parable is obvious. Those so-called foundations are flimsy and unstable. When the storms of life come (and they always do), a life built on sandy soil will crumble to pieces. The career won't last forever. The other person will disappoint us. We lose friends. Our bodies age. No matter how much money we have, we can't take a dime with us when we die.

A life built on any of these foundations will not ultimately stand firm. They will most certainly collapse when we face our final storm, the day when our lungs take in their last breath of air.

However, if we put the teachings of Jesus into practice, it's like building a home on a strong and trustworthy foundation—one that can withstand even the most brutal storms of life. If we trust in Jesus for our salvation, even death cannot destroy us. A life resting on the gospel is strong and secure.

In both Matthew's and Luke's accounts, Jesus did not say, "Whoever hears my words is like a person who has built his house on a rock." Rather, he said, "Whoever hears my words and *puts them into practice*." Throughout the New Testament, we are encouraged to apply what we've learned. Knowledge is not enough. Intellectual assent to certain propositional truths cannot save. A solid foundation doesn't come through memorizing scripture, quoting catechisms, or getting first place in a Bible drill competition.

Rather, the solid foundation is built when we take what we know and apply it to our lives.

The following is a deviation from the other chapters in the book. Rather than turning the ancient parable of Jesus into a modern-day story, this narrative highlights the truth Jesus taught. In it, we see the danger of building our lives on a sandy foundation.

CADEN'S CURVE

Caden Robinson was *raised right,* an expression often used in small, southern towns to describe an individual with parents who worked hard to instill the correct values and morals into their children. Whenever people in Mapleton talked about Caden, this fact always seemed to enter the conversation. Both his mom and dad were Mapleton natives. Derek Robinson and his wife, Julie, started dating when they were juniors at Mapleton High School. Their relationship continued through college. Derek attended Shorter College in Rome, Georgia, while Julie went to Auburn University. They married the summer after graduation and moved to Birmingham. Derek attended law school at Samford University, while Julie supported them both by teaching biology at Homewood High School. Three years later, they moved back to Mapleton. Derek joined the Hilbert, Godwin, and Anderson law firm as an associate, becoming a named partner five years later.

Both Derek and Julie grew up attending the First Baptist Church of Mapleton. When they moved back to their hometown, they once again became active in their church, initially serving as leaders in the youth group, teaching a high school small group, and serving as chaperones on retreats. After the birth of their son, they both volunteered in the preschool ministry and, later, in the children's ministry. Julie also sang in the choir and Derek served as a deacon. To say they were active members of the church was an understatement.

Caden and his younger sister, Claire, had been involved in First Baptist their entire lives. Neither remembered a time when church activities didn't play a central role in their family's schedule.

This is part of the reason people said Caden was *raised right*. The other reason is that there were no two finer people in Mapleton than Derek and Julie Robinson. Once Claire reached middle school, Julie went back to teaching high school biology. She was an instant favorite among the student body. Mrs. Robinson knew how to get teenagers to enjoy biology—an amazing feat in and of itself. However, she was also loved because of her kind and gentle nature. Any student with a problem felt free to talk with Julie. She exuded compassion and understanding, always giving wise counsel to those who found themselves struggling with a decision.

Although Derek kept a full schedule with his legal practice, he prioritized his wife and kids. He never worked on Saturdays, often joking that his kids "owned him" on that day. As well, he coached both of his children in their various sporting endeavors. Derek had been a standout basketball player in high school and was a natural choice to coach Caden's Upward basketball team, then his Little League baseball team, Claire's community center soccer team, and just about any other recreational sports team on which his son or daughter played.

The children who played for him loved Coach Derek. He always encouraged, never demeaned, and the players learned a lot about how to play the sport. The parents adored him as well. He played to win, but not at the expense of benching the less-talented kids. Every player got multiple opportunities to participate in the games, often in several different positions. His teams almost always won the championship at the end of their season.

With parents like that, there was no doubt that Caden had been *raised right.* When people talked about Caden, this fact was almost always mentioned.

However, this was *not* why people talked often about Caden Robinson. His name as a topic of conversation had little to do with the values instilled in him by his parents. Instead, it had everything to do with Caden's skills on the baseball field—specifically, his abilities on the pitching mound. Caden almost singlehandedly managed to elevate baseball to a top-tier sport at Mapleton High School. Previously, the surrounding community largely ignored the high school baseball team. Football games often attracted a couple thousand spectators. Basketball brought about half that number.

Baseball games, however, were only attended by parents, grandparents, and perhaps a handful of girlfriends. Very few without a direct connection to a player came to watch games.

That is, until Caden Robinson joined the team. The kid had a rocket for an arm, consistently throwing an 85

MPH fastball and placing it within a circle the size of a dinner plate.

But even that wasn't what brought so many spectators to games. These fans came to witness his incredible, almost impossible-to-hit curveball. According to head coach Jimmy Jones, he'd never seen a high school pitcher throw a curve with that kind of consistency and control. Caden's typical attack on a right-handed batter began with fastball, a little high and inside. Just enough to rattle the batter, but not anywhere close to hitting him. Then, the next pitch would be a curveball, headed directly at the batter's head. This usually sent him scurrying out of the batter's box and falling to the ground to avoid getting hit—only to hear a loud *thump* in the catcher's mitt followed by the umpire thunderously announcing, "Strike!"

Even when they knew it was coming, batters could not manage to keep their feet planted in the box. The ball appeared to be headed right at them. And yet, nine times out of ten, that seemingly inside pitch managed to cross the middle of the plate. "Ain't ever seen nuthin' like it," Coach Jones repeatedly declared. "Nuthin' like it in all my years coaching."

Hundreds of Mapleton's citizens lined the fences when word spread that Caden would be the starting pitcher. Baseball had previously been a sort of placeholder sport between basketball season and football season. It gave a few of the football players something to do in the spring, at least when they weren't in the weight room.

Caden changed all of that. During his junior year, college scouts came to watch games. Whispers began circulating about him getting a full scholarship to a D1 school. Those same whispers became shouts at the end of the season. Georgia, Georgia Tech, North Carolina, and Tennessee all offered full scholarships to Caden before he began his senior year of high school.

"Where's he gonna go?" was the oft-repeated question.

"His mama and daddy said he hasn't decided yet. He's going to take some time and pray about it. He wants to go wherever the Lord wants him to go."

"That boy sure was raised right, wasn't he?"

To the surprise of no one, Caden Robinson chose the University of Georgia. His grandfather, Robert Robinson, played on Georgia's football team in the late 1960s under then-head coach Vince Dooley. "Poppy" played four years as an offensive lineman, back when the average weight for a college lineman was less than 250 pounds. Caden grew up watching football games on Saturdays with his grandfather, and even traveled to Athens with him a few times each season to be a spectator among the crowd of more than 90,000. Nearly half of Caden's wardrobe consisted of T-shirts, sweatshirts, hats, and other items emblazoned with a UGA logo. While he appreciated the offers from the other schools, he knew he would never be able to pitch with his whole heart against his beloved Bulldogs. He prayed about his decision, but knew the Lord would have to paint a message in the nighttime sky if he wanted Caden to go anywhere else. In his mind, it was the only logical choice.

The Robinson's spent the week of July 4th at Panama City Beach. It was their last family trip before Caden started college. There was a sense of excitement over this next stage in Caden's baseball career, but feelings of sadness as well. Soon, there would be an empty chair at the dinner table. Caden would not be part of their family's daily routine. Derek and Julie put up brave fronts, but secretly they yearned to stop time, perhaps even turn back the clock. Gone were the days of coaching Little League games, throwing in the yard and staying up late to watch the Atlanta Braves.

Claire, as well, would miss her older brother. Two years his junior, he was both her friend and hero. Her friends were jealous of their relationship—how protective he was of her, how he always offered to give her a ride, how he came to watch her play soccer, cheering for her with as much enthusiasm as the crowds cheered for him at baseball games. The only upside to him moving was the fact that her friends might cease asking her to set them up with Caden. Other than that, there was nothing good about him leaving. She would miss her big brother.

On their last night of vacation, Julie and Claire watched a movie while Derek took Caden to an ice cream shop.

"Son, I want you to know how proud I am of you."

"I know, Dad. You've told me that before."

"I've told you more than once because I don't want you to forget it."

"I won't, Dad."

"There's something else I don't want you to forget either. Ever since you started playing T-ball, I have used this phrase with you. However, the truth of what I've told you for all of these years will apply now more than ever. And although you've heard me say it a thousand times before, I hope it's not just white noise to you. Please remember that baseball is a great sport, but…"

"I know, Dad. I've heard you say this my whole life."

"Then please finish the sentence for me."

"Okay, okay. Baseball is a great sport, but an awful god."

"Caden, I know you believe that. But this truth will be put to the test in your life over the coming months and years. You are headed to the big leagues, both literally and figuratively. You may or may not finish at Georgia before you get an offer from an MLB team. I can't guarantee you that will happen, but unless you suddenly forget everything you've learned about pitching, you'll get a professional contract. And I know you're excited about that prospect. It's every Little Leaguer's dream."

"Absolutely, Dad. And I'm tremendously thankful that it's even a possibility."

"Caden, it's more than a possibility. At this point, I'd call it a probability. And I'm thankful for it as well.

However, son, I do worry. You seem to have a great head on your shoulders and a strong walk with the Lord. But the D1 sports world can be a difficult one to navigate. I just need you to remember who you are and whose you are. And that your mom and I love you very much."

"I love you, too, Dad. And thanks so much for the ice cream."

Jessica Banning graduated from Myers Park High School in Charlotte, North Carolina before attending the University of Georgia. Jessica grew up in a solid middle-class family. Her father taught English at the same middle school she attended. Mrs. Banning was a stay-at-home mom. They lived in a modest four-bedroom house on a side street in the Myers Park section of Charlotte. Most of their neighbors lived in much larger homes. Most of Jessica's friends came from families with money. While the Bannings had all they needed, they weren't members of an elite country club, didn't go on skiing vacations to Aspen, and didn't drive the latest cars. In their home, summer was a noun, not a verb. They were fine, but not in the position to enjoy the finer things in life.

Although she was an early childhood education major, her true goal was an "MRS" degree. More specifically, she sought to marry into money, or at least someone who had the potential of making lots of money. Jessica's plan was to escape her childhood economic status and move into a more privileged category.

During her first semester, she met Zach, a first-year student from Albany, Georgia. In her opinion, he checked every box of the perfect boyfriend qualifications. He made her laugh, was kind and thoughtful, called her often but wasn't overly suffocating, and seemed to have many other friends. Plus, Zach was incredibly easy on the eyes. When they went out together, she observed other girls taking notice of her date, sometimes inappropriately staring at him from across a restaurant. Truthfully, it made her smile, knowing how jealous they were of her boyfriend.

They quickly became exclusive, spending Friday and Saturday nights together as well as seeing each other several times during the week.

However, after only a couple of months of dating, their situation suddenly changed. They spent a sunny, fall Saturday afternoon studying together outside on a picnic blanket, enjoying the weather and one another's company. During a break from their reading, Zach opened up to Jessica about his future dreams. He had been a standout high school football player but not quite good enough to play at the college level. However, he was happiest on the football field (although he quickly corrected himself; he was very happy with Jessica right now). His goal was to become a high school physical education teacher and football coach, maybe even one day becoming an athletic director. He dreamed of spending his Friday nights under the lights, on the field, leading boys to do more than they could imagine.

Jessica saw the look in Zach's eyes as he talked about this future hope, and she knew he was right. This would be his path to finding fulfillment. Any other career would not do.

And, sadly, she knew she wouldn't find happiness being a part of his story. Her dream—a lifestyle enjoying the finer things of life—would not be realized as the wife of a high school coach. She liked Zach. A lot. She might have even said she was falling in love with him.

Which is why she had to immediately put an end to their relationship.

It was Jessica's roommate, Lacy, who first told her about Caden Robinson. Lacy started dating a guy on the baseball team—Landon somebody. Landon told Lacy who told Jessica all about a first-year student from Mapleton who was this amazing pitcher with an unbelievable curveball. Jessica wasn't all that interested in the story until Lacy repeated what Landon told her about Caden most likely getting a contract from a major league team in the next year or two, and that he imagined it would come with a signing bonus of $5 million, maybe more. Jessica questioned the veracity of this statement until she went online and did a little research. She even found articles about this top-rated pitcher from Mapleton High School who received a full scholarship to play for UGA. The articles also contained multiple pictures of Caden, both on and off the field. Jessica was impressed. And motivated to find out all she could about Mr. Caden Robinson.

This is why she decided to attend a freshman Bible study that met in a classroom on campus. Jessica had not been raised in a particularly religious family. They went to a Methodist church near their home once or twice a year, typically on Easter and around Christmas. She hadn't thought much about God or Jesus, and she didn't own a Bible. Earlier that day, she went to a bookstore in town and asked to purchase one.

"What version?" the saleslady asked.

"I don't know. I guess the original version," Jessica replied.

"Well, the original version would be in Hebrew and Greek. Are you fluent in either of those languages?"

"Uh, no. I guess I mean the original English version."

"That would be the King James. But, sweetie, it's difficult to read if you're not familiar with that translation. Can I recommend the English Standard Version to you? We have several different colors available."

Jessica showed up to the Bible study that evening with her brand-new Bible in hand. She walked into the classroom alone, appearing to be lost and out of place.

It was precisely how she'd planned it.

Caden's parents instilled in him and his sister the importance of always looking out for someone who needed help. While in high school, Caden never sat with the same group of friends during lunch. Instead, he would look for someone sitting alone, walk over with his tray, and ask if he could join them. Caden's popularity among his classmates was high enough that his actions inspired other students to act less cliquish and more inclusive.

When Caden saw Jessica sitting alone at the back of the room, reading her brand new Bible, his heart went out to her. He excused himself from the group of friends standing around chatting before the Bible study, then walked over and sat down beside Jessica.

"Hey, I'm Caden," he said.

"Jessica," she replied with her friendliest smile.

"You're new here, right?"

"I guess it's that obvious, isn't it? I came to school last fall and did the typical party thing. But, you know, it all left me feeling empty inside. Over the Christmas break, I decided to get serious about my relationship with the Lord. I really don't know any Christians on campus. That's why I came tonight, hoping to study the Bible but to meet some new people as well."

"I'm glad you came, and you're welcome to come over and sit with me and my friends."

"Thanks," she replied as she touched his arm and gave him a flirtatious smile. "You've really made me feel welcome."

Although Jessica had not attended church as a child, she astutely observed Caden and his friends. She then did her best to emulate their practices and speech. When they sang Christian songs at their Bible study, Jessica noticed people around her closing their eyes and raising their hands in the air. She did the same.

When a leader stood on the stage and told the gathered crowd to turn to the book of Galatians, she glanced over at Caden and noticed him flipping to pages near the end of his Bible. She followed suit and breathed a sigh of relief when she found the right page.

They went out to a restaurant after the Bible study. She was about to dive into her food when she observed everyone else waiting. When Caden offered to say the blessing, others bowed their heads. She did the same and quickly learned that this was a standard practice.

She listened carefully to the conversations happening around her, soaking in all the lingo and taking copious mental notes on what these Christian students believed and how they acted.

To avoid talking about herself, Jessica asked the students lots of questions about themselves. This seemingly selfless interest in the lives of others endeared her to Caden and his friends. But, especially to Caden. Jessica was different. She never wanted the spotlight. She always directed the conversation back to others, their lives, their interests, and wanting to hear more about their story.

By the time baseball season began, Caden and Jessica were officially dating. She'd offered a vague testimony of her relationship with the Lord, just enough to appease Caden before she turned the conversation back to him and his story. He loved how Jessica always wanted to hear more about him, his day, and his feelings. She especially loved listening to him talk about baseball and the probability of him playing professionally. Jessica asked him questions, but not in an annoying way. She learned his interests and asked about those things. If he didn't feel like talking, she backed off. She was there for him when he needed her, but never acted like a suffocating girlfriend.

Jessica was, in his mind, truly selfless. Or so he thought.

It was an afternoon home game against the University of South Carolina, and it was Caden's second start as a college player. He'd pitched four great innings, only giving up one hit and keeping the Gamecocks scoreless. With two outs, one strike, and a runner on first, he threw a formidable curveball to a right-handed batter. The ball started high and inside, causing the batter to duck and nearly fall onto the dirt. However, the ball broke hard and dropped across the inside corner, popping into the catcher's mitt and eliciting a called "Strike two!" from the umpire.

The gathered crowd roared with approval. It was Caden Robinson at his finest.

CADEN'S CURVE

The catcher threw the ball back to Caden, who then happened to notice the first base runner drifting a few feet off the bag. As soon as the ball hit his glove, Caden turned and fired hard to the first baseman. The ball arrived before the runner could make a move back to the bag. The first baseman made the tag, and the inning was over.

However, Caden instantly knew something was wrong. When he made the hard throw, he felt something snap in his shoulder. Instantly, pain shot through his right arm and shoulder. As he made his way to the dugout, he realized that he could not lift his arm above his waist without a searing pain shooting through it. He told his coach, who immediately called for the trainer. They wrapped his upper arm and shoulder in an icepack and immediately took him to Northeast Orthopedics.

An Xray and MRI confirmed what Dr. Bradley suspected. Caden had a major tear in his labrum—what is commonly called a "SLAP" tear. The doctor sat on a stool with his hands on his knees as he delivered the news to Caden and Mr. Robinson, both seated in chairs beside one another.

"I hate to tell you this, but I need to be upfront and honest. While physical therapy could help, you really need surgery. And, sadly, your best hope is about an 80% recovery. I try to never say never, but the chances of you pitching again at the college level are slim to none. However, with this surgery, you'll be able to do just about anything else you want to do. As long as what you want to do doesn't involve throwing a 95-mile-per-hour fastball or a curve that breaks three feet."

Derek Robinson reached over and grabbed his son's hand. Tears ran down both of their cheeks.

"What do you mean you'll never pitch again?!?"

They sat on a bench in the lobby of her dorm. Fortunately, it was a Sunday afternoon, and no one else was around. This was a side of Jessica that Caden had never seen. Her sweet, gentle demeanor was completely gone. Caden remembered reading the book, *Dr. Jekyll and Mr. Hyde*, by Robert Louis Stevenson while in high school. That story came to mind as he listened to Jessica interrogate him like a police officer going after a hardened criminal. *I don't like this Mr. Hyde*, he thought. *I want Dr. Jekyll back.*

"What'd you say?!?" she practically yelled at him.

Oops, I guess I accidentally said that out loud, Caden thought.

"Why are you so worked up, Jessica? It is my life and dreams that have been crushed, not yours."

She stared at Caden hard, with a pensive look on her face. Finally, after a few seconds of silence, she held up her hands and said, "You're right. You're exactly right. I'm sorry Caden. I guess I was just so hurt for you that I let it get to me. I just want you to be happy, and I'm sorry this has happened."

"Thanks, Jessica."

"So, just out of curiosity, what do you think you'll do now that your baseball career is, ummm, you know, no longer an option?"

"Yeah, I've been thinking about that a lot. And I'm pretty sure that the Lord is calling me into the ministry. It's something that has always been in the back of my mind. Even when I thought I might play professional baseball, I hoped that ministry might be my second career. Now it looks like it could be my first career."

"Just to be clear—when you say go into the ministry, you mean like a pastor of a church?"

"Uh, yeah, that's one option. Or maybe a youth minister. I really don't know all the details at this point."

"You know, there was this girl in my high school. Her father was some kind of associate pastor at a church in Charlotte. I don't remember the details of what her dad did, but I do remember that she drove a really junky car. And didn't seem to have very expensive clothes or jewelry. I mean, our family didn't have much, but they really seemed to struggle financially."

"Well, Jessica, a pastor certainly isn't going to make as much as a professional baseball player. But money isn't everything. I know people who aren't rich but they're very happy. My goal in life doesn't center on how much money I can make."

Jessica sat there, looking at Caden with that same pensive expression. Her wheels were turning, carefully considering her next words. Finally, she broke the silence.

"Mine does."

"What?"

"My goal does center on money. I don't plan to spend the rest of my life struggling to make ends meet. I want to be able to afford a big house, nice cars, exciting vacations." Her voice trailed off before pausing, then looking down and away from Caden. "I just can't see myself married to a pastor. For so many reasons. I'm not saying we were going to get married, but there's certainly no point in us continuing to date if, you know, we have different goals in life."

Caden sat, somewhat dumbfounded, but with an unusual peace in his heart. The next words from his mouth surprised him but felt exactly right. "I understand, Jessica. I wish you the best. I really do."

Then he got up and walked out of her dorm and her life forever.

Two years later, Caden turned a corner in the Tate Student Center and unexpectedly came face to face with Jessica Banning. They had not seen one another since that day in her dorm. Caden almost didn't recognize her; Jessica somehow looked different. It wasn't her hair color or style, although it was slightly shorter and blonder than when they were dating. It was something about her eyes. They looked tired. Or maybe sad. He wondered if she was just having a bad day.

"Well, hey, Jessica. It's been a long time. Are you okay?"

"I'm fine," she quickly replied. "Well, not really, but you're not interested in my junk."

"That's not true. I'm sorry to hear this. What's going on?"

"My boyfriend and I broke up. He's such a jerk. He thinks just because his daddy has tons of money that he can do whatever…" She stopped, suddenly remembering their conversation from a couple of years before. A wave of guilt washed over her as she thought about the reason she ended her relationship with Caden. Now, she looked back at her choices and realized how foolish they'd been. The desire for wealth and the supposed happiness and security it brought had led her down a bad path. The money dream had been nothing but a mirage.

She sighed and said, "You know, I really don't want to talk about it. But I do want to know about you. I heard you were back pitching for the baseball team."

"Yeah, it turned out that the first diagnosis was way off. I had a slight tear, but it wasn't nearly as bad as the doctor originally thought. I did lots of physical therapy, and I'm back on the team. Well, that's not exactly true. This past week, I played my last game for the University of Georgia."

"Really? What happened? Did you get cut?"

Caden laughed. "Not exactly. I got a contract with the Atlanta Braves."

QUESTIONS FOR DISCUSSION:

Ice-Breaker: Have you purchased something you thought was well-made, only to discover it wasn't? Describe that experience.

1. What are some similarities between this story and the parable of Jesus? Differences?
2. Read Matthew 7:21-23. These words of Jesus appear just before the parable of the wise and foolish builders. They are strong words. How can we do a lot of things for Jesus, but miss the mark of following him?
3. Read Luke 6:47-49. This is the same parable Jesus told in Matthew; however, Luke adds the following introduction by Jesus: "Why do you call me 'Lord, Lord' and do not do what I say?" How does that fit in with the point Jesus made in the parable?
4. For those religious leaders listening to Jesus, the foundation upon which they had built their lives was their ability to follow the law. Why was and is this a sandy foundation?
5. Read James 1:22-25. What do these verses say about knowledge versus application of the word?
6. Read John 14:15. What did Jesus mean by these words? If we do not always perfectly obey the commands of Jesus, does that mean we do not love him?
7. How does the application of God's word in our lives serve as a strong foundation?

QUESTIONS FOR DISCUSSION:

8. Can you think of a time when you have faced a storm or storms, but the application of God's word kept your life from crumbling?

CHAPTER 8
MAPLETON'S MURDER
The Parable of the Tenant Farmers

Jesus then began to speak to them in parables: "A man planted a vineyard. He put a wall around it, dug a pit for the winepress and built a watchtower. Then he rented the vineyard to some farmers and moved to another place. At harvest time he sent a servant to the tenants to collect from them some of the fruit of the vineyard. But they seized him, beat him and sent him away empty-handed. Then he sent another servant to them; they struck this man on the head and treated him shamefully. He sent still another, and that one they killed. He sent many others; some of them they beat, others they killed.

"He had one left to send, a son, whom he loved. He sent him last of all, saying, 'They will respect my son.'

"But the tenants said to one another, 'This is the heir. Come, let's kill him, and the inheritance will be ours.' So they took him and killed him, and threw him out of the vineyard.

"What then will the owner of the vineyard do? He will come and kill those tenants and give the vineyard to others. Haven't you read this passage of Scripture:

*"'The stone the builders rejected
has become the cornerstone;*

the Lord has done this,
and it is marvelous in our eyes'?"

Then the chief priests, the teachers of the law and the elders looked for a way to arrest him because they knew he had spoken the parable against them. But they were afraid of the crowd; so they left him and went away.

Mark 12:1-12

A Few Comments...

This parable appears in all three synoptic gospels (Matthew 21, Mark 12, and Luke 20). Jesus told this story just days before he was crucified and shortly after he had overturned the moneychangers table in the temple. Up to this point, the religious leaders had tolerated the ministry of Jesus. His popularity among the masses meant they had to put up with his unorthodox manner of teaching and his propensity for spending time with tax collectors and sinners. On numerous occasions, the religious leaders attempted to trap Jesus with a question, hoping his answer would anger or disappoint those in the crowd. However, every effort to outwit Jesus failed spectacularly, always elevating Jesus in the eyes of the crowd. Therefore, the priests and teachers hesitated to attack Jesus directly, fearing the inevitable backlash that would come from the people.

But flipping the moneychangers' table put a bullseye squarely on Jesus. The chief priests and other religious leaders now had a new determination to rid the world of this man. In their eyes, he was a menace, a troublemaker, and perhaps even an insurrectionist. It was time to deal with Jesus.

According to Mark's account, these priests, teachers, and elders approached Jesus with a question. I imagine them moving like an amoeba, this single-celled mob, approaching Jesus with scowling faces. A spokesman for the group asked Jesus, "By what authority do you do these things?"

Jesus, as was often his custom, answered their question with another question. "Tell me, by what authority did John perform baptisms? Was this from heaven, or from men?"

Rats, they thought. *Jesus has trapped us again. If we say, "from heaven," Jesus will ask why we didn't believe him. If we say, "from men," all the people will be angry because they believed John was a prophet.*

"Umm, we don't know," their spokesman replied.

"Then I will not tell you by what authority I do these things. However, would you be interested in hearing a story?"

Jesus began this parable by describing a familiar setting. In the first century, it was typical for a wealthy individual to purchase land and live there long enough to prepare the soil and plant crops, hire tenants to care for the farm or vineyards, and then move elsewhere. When harvest time came, this landowner would send a servant to collect his portion of the proceeds.

In this parable, the tenant farmers beat the first servant, struck the second, and killed the third. The landowner sent more servants, and all were treated in similar ways. This wealthy person eventually decided to send his son, thinking that his son would get respect from the farmers. However, the farmers killed the son, believing the land would become theirs with the son out of the picture.

The immediate application of this parable could not be more apparent. The landowner is God, the farmers are the nation of Israel, the servants represent the prophets sent by God over the centuries, and the son is, obviously, Jesus. In this story, Jesus condemned the Jews for the ways in which they rejected God's prophets, often ignoring, or beating, or sometimes killing these men. Moreover, he predicted his own death at the hands of these religious leaders—a prophecy fulfilled only a few days later.

Again, the immediate application of this parable is clear. After his death, the kingdom of God quickly moved away from Israel and into the Gentile world.

However, there is application for us. When you read these accounts, the religious leaders are amazingly unrepentant and stiff-necked. There is zero openness to correction or consideration of their actions.

How often are we the same way? This chapter's small group discussion questions will focus on our posture before God and others, specifically when we face correction. Are we humble and open, or proud and obstinate?

Now, for the final chapter and a dramatic event in the history of Mapleton, Georgia.

MAPLETON'S MURDER

Robert Peek, Jr.—called Robby by everyone who knew him—was 22 years old when he went to work for his father at the First National Bank of Grant County. Wanting to avoid any rumors of nepotism and desiring even more to teach his son a few lessons about hard work and merit-based rewards, Mr. Peek put Robby through every interview and test given to all applicants. However, it was incredibly obvious that Robby was the most qualified individual to seek employment at First National in several years. Not hiring Robby would be unfair to him and to the bank. Mr. Peek hired his son as an entry-level employee.

Eleven years later, Robby held the title of First Vice-President. Mr. Peek, at 62 years of age, was seriously considering retirement and felt confident that his son could step into his shoes. Robby had proven himself to be more than capable in handling money and people. First National Bank would be in good hands under Robby's leadership.

As well, Mr. Peek knew that he and his wife had raised Robby with the right values. Throughout high school, he stayed out of trouble, made good grades, and ran in the right social circles. He was accepted to the University of Georgia, joined a fraternity, again managed to stay out of trouble, majored in finance, graduated *cum laude*, and returned to his hometown. That summer, Robby married a girl he met during his junior year at a sorority mixer. She grew up in the Johns Creek area of Atlanta where her father worked as an orthopedic surgeon.

Mr. Peek could not have been any prouder.

Robby became known around Mapleton as an honest banker and all-around good guy. Married with two young children at home, a member of First Baptist Church, and active in several community groups, Robby really was a model citizen of Grant County.

Robby was also an avid runner, finally deciding at 33 years old to train for a marathon. This goal led Robby into a friendship that would dramatically change his life.

Henry Miller had served as the pastor of First Baptist Church since 1997. Running long distances was the primary way he relieved stress and mentally worked through both personal and church-related issues. At this point in his life, he had three marathon medals in his possession: the Marine Corps Marathon in Washington, D.C., the Thanksgiving Day Marathon in Atlanta, Georgia, and the Rock and Roll Marathon in Nashville, Tennessee.

Henry now had his sights set on qualifying for the Boston Marathon. To achieve this goal, he had to complete another marathon in under three hours and ten minutes. Two years earlier, he ran the Marine Corps Marathon in three hours and thirteen minutes. He'd missed qualifying by only three minutes, and a pulled hamstring kept him from running another race that year.

This year, however, he was committed to putting in the training hours necessary for this goal to become a reality. On most Monday, Tuesday, and Thursday afternoons, Henry left the church office at five o'clock, ran up Main Street and followed a predetermined route that would eventually lead him back to the church parking lot and his waiting car.

On this particular Tuesday, he returned to First Baptist after finishing a ten-mile run in 71 minutes—his best time so far at this distance. As he walked around the corner of the church education building, he noticed Robby Peek standing next to his car. Robby and his family attended worship services at First Baptist sporadically, mainly around Easter, Christmas, Mother's Day, and perhaps on a few other occasions during the year. Henry knew Robby, primarily through the church's business dealings with First National Bank. However, they certainly weren't close friends. Henry was surprised to see Robby standing there, apparently waiting on Henry, and silently wondered if something was wrong.

"Hey, Robby. Is everything okay?"

"Yeah, Pastor Henry. I saw you running up Main earlier and figured you would end up back here. It looked like you had a great pace. How far did you run?"

"Ten miles. I'm trying to qualify for the Boston Marathon. I've signed up for the Albany Marathon in

September. I hear it's a flat course. I hope to have a good race if it's not too hot that day."

"Yeah, Pastor, that's why I wanted to come talk to you. I heard you were planning on running the Albany race, and, well, I've also signed up for it. I just need someone to train with me."

"Have you done a marathon before?"

"No, only a half. The Thanksgiving Day race in Atlanta. But I ran it in just under an hour and a half."

"Really? That's pretty good."

"Thanks, but I've never trained for a marathon before, and I need help. And someone to hold me accountable. You're the only guy in town I know who is currently training for a marathon."

Pastor Henry thought for a minute. The truth is, he was going to say "yes" to Robby. He really wanted to train with a partner. However, he decided to use this opportunity for something more than just physical growth. "Robby," he said, "I'll do it on one condition. You meet me for breakfast, once a week, for the next three months. You pick the morning—any day except Saturday or Sunday. We can get together at the All-American Cafe. Tommy McClendon has a small room in the back he lets me use from time to time for private meetings. What I'd like to do is to buy you breakfast and then spend thirty minutes going through a book of the Bible. In fact, Robby, I'll even let you pick the book we study together."

Robby had not seen this coming at all. He and his family attended worship at First Baptist fairly often, he thought to himself. Well, not that often, but if they were in town or weren't too tired or if none of the kids were sick, they went. Maybe a couple of times per month? No, that's not right. As he thought about it, he remembered that Easter was the last time they attended. Now, it was the first week of May. They really were sporadic in their attendance. He knew he needed to change that.

But as far as the breakfast deal went, why not? He genuinely liked Pastor Henry, and he sure needed a running partner. Plus, he probably could use a little Bible study in his life.

"Uh, okay, sounds good. Can we do Wednesday mornings at 7:00 a.m.? I just need to be in the office by 8:30 a.m. And I really have no idea what book of the Bible to study. Can you just choose one?"

"I'm happy to do that, Robby. So, I'll see you in the morning at 7:00 a.m.?"

"Wait, you mean we start this week?"

"Why not? Do you have any conflicts in the morning?"

"Well, uh…" Robby couldn't think of anything on his calendar, and he hated to lie to the Pastor. "Uh, I guess not. I'll see you in the morning."

Henry chose the New Testament book of Philippians for their study. At their first meeting together, Robby shared that he had grown up attending Sunday School and worship services about as sporadically as his own family now attended. He had, however, made what he considered a genuine profession of faith in Christ when he was in middle school. A Sunday School teacher shared the gospel on a day Robby happened to attend. After class, Robby asked the teacher if he could hang back and talk for a minute. They did, and Robby ended up praying to receive Christ that morning.

The following Sunday, Robby was baptized. He was excited about his newfound faith in Christ. Robby begged his parents to go each Sunday. For a while, they became more active than they'd ever been. However, a few weeks later, his summer became busy with vacations, baseball, visits to his grandparents' home in Atlanta, and a host of other activities.

"We just got out of the routine," he said. "That fall, we returned to our normal schedule of attending only occasionally. But my prayer way back then was real, and I've never forgotten about it. I try to pray every morning and to treat others the way I would want to be treated. I guess I've just fallen into the same pattern as my parents, letting busyness get in the way of my church attendance and relationship with the Lord."

Henry listened and nodded, noticing that Robby had hardly touched his breakfast, while he'd nearly finished his own.

"But, Pastor, I'm working on changing that. I'll be in church on Sundays; if I'm not, you have my permission to ask me why. And don't let me give you some weak excuse. Unless I'm sick or out of town, expect to see my smiling face."

Two months later, on a Saturday morning, Henry and Robby finished a 15-mile run and returned to First Baptist Church. It was only 9:00 a.m. and already 83 degrees. Plus, the humidity was stifling. Both were drinking Gatorade, trying to rehydrate after a nearly two-hour run.

They sat on a bench just outside the main entrance to the church sanctuary, discussing their time, pace, and strategy to shave just a few more seconds off each mile before the marathon. After a thorough analysis of their training, Robby cleared his throat and spoke with a serious tone.

"Pastor, I need you to know something. First, I appreciate you allowing me to run with you. I would not have been able to train for a marathon without your guidance and encouragement."

"But honestly, this Wednesday morning Bible study has been even more beneficial. It's the exact kick in the pants I needed to get serious about my spiritual life. I've been reading the Bible daily; my conversations with my wife have been different; my thoughts and desires are now different; and, as you know, we have been in church every Sunday since you and I first met at All-American."

"Robby, I'm thrilled to hear all of this. Believe it or not, your passion for the Lord has inspired me. Even as a pastor, I sometimes get on cruise control in my spiritual walk, especially when I feel like my ministry isn't making a difference. There are Sundays I'll preach, and I look out over a congregation of people who seem to be completely disinterested. Of course, I worry that it's just my preaching, but I am honestly more concerned that they are just bored with the Lord."

"I understand what you mean, Pastor Henry. And that's why I wanted to talk to you. You see, I might can help you change that. Before our conversation a few months ago, I was one of those apathetic people you saw in the congregation. It wasn't that I was opposed to reading my Bible or praying or coming to worship. Those things just weren't my priority. So, when I did come to church, well, I guess I wasn't fully engaged."

"But when you asked me to do more, I was completely open to the idea. And I think others will be as well."

"So, here is my proposal. I'd like to spend the next three months talking with men in our church and encourage them in a similar way. I don't have all the details worked out yet, but I believe it could change some lives, much like mine did. What do you think, Pastor?"

Over the next few weeks, their conversations centered around Robby's idea. After much prayer and discussion, they decided to challenge men in their church to a "No Shave November." During this time, men were encouraged to grow their beards as a sign of their commitment to wholeheartedly pursue the Lord. Henry and Robby determined that this pledge would include the following:

- Read a chapter each day from the book of Proverbs.
- Attend worship each Sunday unless providentially hindered.
- Faithfully giving a tithe to the church.
- Meet with a group of men during the week to pray for the church.

They also determined that this would not be an official church initiative. There would be no banners on the church website or announcements in worship. Rather, Henry and Robby would personally ask men to commit and, if they agreed, encourage them to invite others to accept the challenge. Robby believed this would be far more effective than an all-call from Pastor Henry.

And he was right. They spent August, September, and October making their individual appeals to men in the church. Those who agreed asked others. And those asked more men to join them. Like a pyramid marketing plan, the commitments grew exponentially. First Baptist—and the city of Mapleton—were about to be forever changed.

In September, Henry and Robby ran the Albany marathon. They stayed together throughout the race, crossing the finish line at the exact same time: three hours and three minutes. Henry finally had the qualifying time he needed for the Boston Marathon.

For three months, Henry and Robby focused their attention only on those associated with First Baptist Church. However, many of those who agreed to take the challenge then invited men who attended other churches in Mapleton. And then they asked others, and the *No Shave November* initiative spread rapidly throughout Grant County. Men quit shaving before the start of the challenge to show their support. Worship attendance steadily increased in virtually every church in Mapleton. *No Shave November* became the number one topic of conversation in diners, offices, and social clubs. However, it was never publicly announced by any pastor or worship leader. No articles about the initiative were printed in any bulletin or church newsletter. As intended, this movement remained a grassroots effort. As such, it continued to gain momentum and influence among the men living in Grant County.

On the first Sunday in November, churches all over Mapleton were packed. According to most pastors, their attendance was higher that day than any other Sunday in the year, including Easter. The same pastors also commented on the strange sight of looking out over a congregation and seeing so many bearded men.

"When I got up to preach, I felt like I'd driven a DeLorean back to 1882," Pastor Henry joked to his wife, Grace. "But, you know, those faces with beards were hanging on to every word I said. I've not experienced anything quite like this in all my years serving this church. And I've seen firsthand that if you can get the men to church, the women and children will follow. You know how often I've complained about wives coming to church, dragging their children while their husbands stay at home or go out to the golf course. Well, this certainly wasn't the case on Sunday. I didn't see a single man dragging his children to church while his wife slept in or went to play golf. I saw families all sitting together and many women with big smiles on their faces."

That November, churches across the county experienced revival. One pastor called it the "Grant County Awakening." Although some cynics predicted that church attendance would wane after the first week, they were magnificently wrong. Every week in November, the beards and the crowds grew. The Sunday after Thanksgiving—usually a low week for churches—was the highest of the month for most. Throughout the county, men, women, teenagers, and children accepted Christ, read their Bibles, formed small groups, and became serious about running hard after Jesus.

The movement continued into December. Attendance remained strong. Financial gifts to churches in November and December were the highest on record. Throughout Mapleton, most residents said it was the best Christmas ever.

Most, but not all.

Wally, Bernard, and Jesse Easom lived within 500 yards of each another in Burnt Hill, an unincorporated community on the east side of Grant County. Their mother and father had the three brothers in rapid succession: Wally, then Bernard a year later, and Jesse one year after that. Now all in their early 60s, these brothers operated their business and their personal lives virtually unhindered by any outside influences. Some residents of Grant County referred to them as the unofficial leaders of the Burnt Hill Mafia, although in reality, the Easom brothers and their sons were the only members of this gang.

Officially, they worked as self-employed carpenters. Unofficially, Easom Brothers Construction was nothing more than a front for their real business: crystal meth, marijuana, and moonshine.

None of the three managed to graduate from high school; however, they clearly understood the importance of market diversification. They sold cheap moonshine to the old-timers. Stills that had been on their property for decades supplied this "white lightning" purchased by good ole' boys from Grant and several surrounding counties.

Marijuana was a recreational drug sold to middle and upper-class teenagers and young adults. This clientele differed greatly from the moonshine customers. They often showed up in German-made vehicles, wearing designer polo shirts, khakis, and topsider shoes. The moonshine buyers came in rusted trucks, wearing thrift store clothes and no shoes.

However, in recent years, crystal meth had become their cash cow. While manufacturers typically used ephedrine-based cold medications to produce meth, this method became increasingly costly and difficult as drug companies and pharmacies regulated the sales of these products. The Easom brothers discovered other commonly used products could be cooked into crystal form and produce a similar euphoric feeling. The availability and low costs of these goods gave them an edge over their competition, especially during the Great Recession years. Lye, acetone, and sulfuric acid were their go-to ingredients, always cut with baking soda. Sure, these chemicals were potentially fatal. Minimally, they created long-term health issues for their users. But most didn't care. These buyers were intense. They needed a cheap, strong drug, and that's exactly what they got with the Easom brothers' products.

Key to their success was the nearly 100 acres of land they owned in the Burnt Hill community. Except for State

Highway 13, cutting straight through the middle of their property, the various sections of their land were only accessible by dirt roads, all winding and many washed out. The best of these roads led to Wally's home—a triple-wide trailer located roughly two miles off the main highway. Smaller, dirt routes extended from his home to Bernard's and Jesse's.

There were, as well, a network of paths snaking through their property. The Easom brothers knew these small trails like the backs of their hands. It was, after all, the place they'd lived their entire lives. And it was, by God, *their* land.

Except, in reality, it wasn't just *their* land. First National Bank of Grant County held the deed to the land as collateral on the $500,000 mortgage secured by all three brothers in 2012. Mr. Peek had major reservations at the time about loaning the Easom brothers half a million dollars. For one, he seriously doubted their ability to repay the loan. More concerning, however, was their source of income. They wrote on their mortgage application that they were self-employed carpenters, but Robert Peek and every other citizen of Grant County knew these brothers did very little work with hammers and saws.

However, when the appraiser estimated the value of the timber on the land to be nearly $600,000, Mr.

Peek decided to move ahead. For six years, the Easom brothers faithfully paid what they owed. Every month, Wally Easom walked into First National Bank and made the $2,800 mortgage payment in cash. While unusual, this violated no laws or banking regulations. As long as he paid the monthly note, Mr. Peek really did not care whether it came by cash or check.

January was the first month Wally did not walk into the bank to make payment on the note. In February, the bank mailed to the Easom brothers a late notice along with the additional amount due because of the late payment.

By the end of February, it was apparent that the Easoms would fail to make another payment in a timely manner. The bank sent another late payment notice. By March, the Easoms owed nearly $9,000 to First National Bank yet, once again, they made no payment. This time, the bank mailed a statement and a foreclosure notice. If the Easom brothers had not contacted the bank to negotiate a payment plan by the end of March, foreclosure proceedings would begin.

On Friday, March 29—the last business day of the month—Wally Easom entered First National Bank just before 9:00 a.m. and asked the teller if he could meet with Mr. Peek. "He's not here," she replied. "He no longer works on Fridays since he's retiring at the end of the year. His son, Robby, is here. Would you like to meet with him?"

"Yeah, I guess that'll have to do." Five minutes later, Robby exited his office and offered a hand to the waiting Mr. Easom. Wally reluctantly accepted the handshake, and then Robby invited him into his office. Once both men were seated, Robby asked Mr. Eason how he could be of assistance.

"Well, you see, we have a loan with your daddy's bank that we took out years ago to pay off some other debts and buy some equipment we needed for our business. I've made payments on that loan now for the last six years, not missing one payment."

"Until this past January, right?" Robby asked.

Wally glared at Robby, squinting his eyes like he was ready to ring his neck. "Yeah," he replied in a gruff tone, "until January. You see, something happened in this county last fall that really affected our business. And from what I hear, you were the primary reason it occurred. So, the way I see it, you're the one to blame for me not being able to come in here and make my mortgage payment."

Robby knew exactly what Wally Easom meant. Individuals all over Grant County had turned to Jesus and, in the process, gave up their alcohol and drug habits. Some claimed to be instantly healed of their addition. Others went into treatment. Regardless, the countless lives changed by the gospel had a direct impact on the Easom brothers' drug and moonshine business. They had fewer customers, which was why Wally had been unable to make the mortgage payment for the past three months.

However, Robby wasn't going to let on that he knew the real reason behind the Easom's current cash flow dilemma. He held up his hands in mock defense. "Hold on, Mr. Easom. I assume you're talking about the *No Shave November* initiative and the effect it's had on men and families in this town. And you're right; Pastor Henry and I were the ones to first extend this challenge. But you and your brothers have a carpentry business. I do not see the connection between this revival and your lack of customers."

Wally stared angrily at Robby. He knew that Robby knew, yet neither could actually say what they both understood as the truth. "Let's just put it this way, Mr. Peek. When everybody gets all excited about Jesus, they lose interest in doing any remodeling. So, you're the reason we ain't had much business lately. And since this is your daddy's bank and will soon be your bank, from what I understand, you need to cut us some slack here. Maybe, you know, delay any required payments until all this Jesus stuff settles down."

There was no way Robby would offer any extension. He wanted Wally Easom and his brothers to either get saved or get gone. Their business had done irreparable damage to the population of Grant County. Their community would be a much better place without them. And since Robby could see that Wally had about zero interest in the gospel, he decided to be clear and straightforward with him.

"Look, Mr. Easom, that's just not going to happen. I'll give you until the end of April to make four payments and late fees. If you fail to pay in full, I will have no choice but to begin the foreclosure process on your land."

"Can I talk to your daddy about this?"

"My dad is retiring at the end of this year. He's leaving these decisions to me since I'm the one who will be living with the future consequences."

"Is there someone else I can talk to? Someone who might be able to override your decision?"

"I'm afraid not, Mr. Easom. As long as I'm here, this is all you've got." Robby reached over and grabbed his stainless-steel tumbler, filled with coffee. He took a sip and placed it back on the corner of his desk, hoping Wally Easom would wrap up this conversation and let him get back to work.

"Well, you see, Mr. Peek, I don't think you're following the terms of the agreement. I need to review the loan documents to be sure you've got the right to foreclose."

"I assure you that I do. I've looked at thousands of loan documents in my career. I'm sure yours is no different."

"Well, maybe it is. I need a copy of it so I can read it myself."

"The bank's copy is in the file room. I don't keep those here in my office."

"Then, Mr. Peek, why don't you go to the file room and get it and make a copy? I'll wait right here."

Robby let out an exasperated sigh as he rose from his chair and walked out of his office and over to the file room. He searched through the cabinet marked "D-F," and quickly located the Easom documents. Robby walked over to Anna Baldwin, who was finishing up with a customer, and asked her to make copies of the file. Robby then returned to his office, where he discovered Wally Easom no longer seated in a chair but standing by the corner of his desk.

"I've got someone making copies of the loan documents," Robby said. "It'll be just a few minutes. You can wait in the lobby."

"Never mind. I think I have a copy at my house." Wally then walked out of Robby's office and exited the bank.

The next couple of hours at First National Bank were incredibly busy. Friday mornings typically were. Customers came to cash paychecks or to make payments. Robby met with five different clients and even assisted the drive-through teller when the line of cars grew long.

It wasn't until 11:30 a.m. that he finally had a chance to sit at his desk and answer a few emails. As he did, he remembered the tumbler of coffee he'd fixed at his house that morning. He'd felt a headache coming on, the caffeine withdrawal effect. Hopefully, he could finish drinking his coffee and get ahead of the pounding in his temples. If not, it was going to be a long afternoon. He took his last sip of coffee just before noon while reading and responding to emails.

At 12:30 p.m., Anna Baldwin knocked on Robby's office door. Hearing nothing, she turned the knob and cracked open the door. "Uh, Mr. Peek, can you come help us? The lunchtime rush is bad right now." As Anna opened the door a little more, she saw Robby on the floor next to his desk. She rushed over to him and screamed for someone to call 911. The paramedics arrived only seven minutes later, but it didn't matter.

Robby Peek was dead.

The autopsy revealed high levels of flunitrazepam in Robby's system. The pathologist explained to the police investigator that these pills, most commonly called "roofies," produce a relaxed, euphoric feeling, lower inhibitions, and impair judgment. They had been used by men who would drop a pill into a date's drink, significantly reducing her ability to resist physical advances.

This drug also lowers the heart rate and suppresses respiratory function. According to the pathologist, Robby had enough of this drug in his system to stop his heart. The autopsy revealed zero evidence of long-term use of this or any other drug. Although he could not say with absolute certainty, the pathologist guessed that Robby didn't take the drug voluntarily.

Plus, these pills were extremely difficult to obtain. They were white, colorless, and odorless, which is why men used them to take advantage of their dates. "This white pill dropped into a drink would never be noticed.

Therefore, a couple of decades ago, pharmaceutical companies began including blue dye in manufacturing these pills. No trace of that dye was found in Robby's system. Somebody used the old-fashioned ones on him. You find anyone with white roofies in their possession, and you'll find Robby's killer."

The investigator agreed. The police did a thorough fingerprint search of Robby's office. They interviewed every person who had been in the bank that morning, including Wally Easom. He was their prime suspect, but they had nothing linking him directly to the crime. They secured a warrant to search his home, his vehicles, and his land. However, they found nothing illegal. No drugs, no weapons, and nothing even remotely suspicious. With no direct physical evidence, the investigation reached a dead end. Unless new information surfaced, the police could not move forward.

Six months after Robby's death, Pastor Henry Miller decided to hold a special Wednesday night prayer service at First Baptist. This evening, there would be no food served, no children's activities, no youth programming, and no choir rehearsal. Rather, it would be a time of focused, intense prayer. Pastor Henry welcomed everyone and voiced the first prayer, but others quickly made their way to the microphones and offered their own prayers. Some prayed for lost friends. A few others prayed for God's people to live out their faith with greater boldness. Most people, though, prayed for the Lord's justice. The vicious murder of Robby Peek was at the forefront of their minds. His name was voiced more than once. Those gathered were still troubled over this tragedy. They ached for his wife, his children, and his parents. Their community had lost one of the good ones. And everyone knew who had committed this awful act, even if the police didn't have sufficient evidence to prove it. They prayed that the Lord would somehow give them the peace to live with this awful injustice.

Those in attendance later described experiencing a palpable sense of God's presence in the sanctuary. Later that evening, Henry told Grace that he'd never been involved in a prayer service filled with so many holy moments. "The sanctuary became a thin place. What I mean is that the divide between heaven and earth became really thin, even if just for a little while. God's up to something. I don't know what it is, but he's definitely up to something."

That same night, Wally, Bernard, and Jesse met in their "business cabin" located deep within their property. This was their private place, its existence only known by the three brothers. A small, almost unidentifiable trail led from a narrow dirt road to this cabin. The structure was surrounded by trees and brush and was virtually undetectable from more than ten yards away in any direction. Cameras with night-vision capabilities were placed on each corner, run by large batteries. If an unsuspecting hunter happened to stumble upon the cabin, he would soon find one of the Easom brothers riding up on a four-wheeler with shotgun in hand, demanding the hunter quickly move away from their property.

However, this never happened. Only the three Easom brothers had ever laid eyes on their secret place.

The cabin had no windows and was always securely locked. A ductless mini-split air conditioner and heat pump, powered by an outside generator, allowed these brothers to conduct their business in complete secrecy. In fact, their unspoken rule was that this was the only place where they would talk about the details of their dealings, and all three brothers had to be present for these discussions.

On the floor of the cabin, under a rug and table, was a large compartment hidden beneath the floorboards. There, the Easom brothers held their most valuable drugs, weapons, and cash inside metal boxes, although the cash boxes were empty at this particular moment.

Wally explained to his brothers that the untimely death of Robby Peek had bought them a little bit of relief on the foreclosure issue. Mr. Peek, completely overcome with grief, had failed to file the proper paperwork. However, Wally had checked their P.O. Box earlier that day, and they had received an official notice from First

National. The Easoms had until the end of the month to pay what was owed, or the bank would begin the process of foreclosing on their 100 acres.

As they discussed their next steps, they listened to the sound of thunder rumbling in the distance. Soon after, the wind began to whip through the trees. "I guess we might be stuck here for a while," Jesse commented. "At least until this storm passes."

The National Weather Service later classified the tornado as an F4, reaching wind speeds estimated at nearly 175 miles per hour. It roared over Grant County and touched down on the eastern side, leveling almost every tree in a stretch of land nearly half a mile long and 200 yards wide. It then raced back to the sky and eventually dissipated. Initial reports declared that the citizens of Grant County were fortunate that this massive tornado caused no loss of life.

However, on that Thursday, emergency crews inspecting the area discovered the bodies of three brothers, Wally, Bernard, and Jesse Easom, each located hundreds of yards away from the others. As well, the authorities came across the floor of what appeared to be a two-room cabin. The walls and roof were destroyed and scattered in multiple directions. All that remained was a compartment hidden under the floorboards of the cabin. Inside were guns, empty metal boxes, and enough drugs to supply the entire population of Grant County.

Also discovered were three bottles of full of Rohypnol pills.

All white.

QUESTIONS FOR DISCUSSION:

Ice-Breaker: Can you think of a time when someone addressed a sin or shortcoming in your life? How did you respond?

1. What are some similarities between this story and the parable of Jesus? Differences?
2. In the story, the Easom brothers faced God's judgment for Wally's crime of killing the son of the bank owner. In the parable of Jesus, the religious leaders faced God's judgment for killing God's son. What are the ways in which God judges those who are against him?
3. Are Christians subject to God's judgment? Why or why not?
4. Read Revelation 3:19-20. How does God treat those he loves? What is the difference between discipline and judgment?
5. Read 2 Corinthians 5:10. The word "judgment seat" in this passage is literally the word "Bema." It was a place in the downtown part of cities in the Roman Empire where those who were enemies of Rome were condemned and those who were friends of Rome were commended. What does this tell you about the meaning of this verse?
6. Read Proverbs 15:31-33. What does this verse say about how we should deal with correction?
7. Read Matthew 18:15-18. According to Jesus, what

is the right process when addressing someone who has sinned against you?
8. Read Proverbs 27:6. Why is it important to be open to rebuke from a friend? Are there friends in your life who have the freedom to do this for you?